Kids' Games

Kids' Games

Traditional Indoor and Outdoor Activities
for Children of All Ages

PHIL WISWELL

DOUBLEDAY

NEW YORK   LONDON   TORONTO   SYDNEY   AUCKLAND

Published by DOUBLEDAY, a division of Bantam Doubleday Dell Publishing Group, Inc., 666 Fifth Avenue, New York, New York 10103.

DOUBLEDAY and the portrayal of an anchor with a dolphin are trademarks of Doubleday, a division of Bantam Doubleday Dell Publishing Group, Inc.

Dedicated to Christine, John, David, and Deirdre
with all the love I've ever felt.

LIBRARY OF CONGRESS CATALOGING-IN-PUBLICATION DATA
Wiswell, Phil.
Kids' games.
Includes index.
Summary: Instructions for playing 130 traditional indoor and outdoor games for children five to fifteen. Includes word games, number and dice games, guessing and memory games, card games, strategy games, solitaire games, and puzzles.
I. Games—Juvenile literature. [I. Games] I. Title.
GV1203.W753   1987   793.4   86-23955
ISBN 0-385-23405-8
Copyright © 1987 by The Learning Annex®
ALL RIGHTS RESERVED
PRINTED IN THE UNITED STATES

4   6   8   9   7   5
MUR

CONTENTS

INTRODUCTION

"Mommy? How do you play ring-o-levio?" . . . "Daddy? Can you play sprouts with me? I forget how to play." . . . "Grandma, can you teach us how to play marbles?"

Kids love to play many kinds of games, and they must rely on parents and elders to teach them the rules. Yet, how many parents remember the hundreds of different games they may have played as children? And how many can accurately describe all the rules? What would you do if a child asked you one of the above questions?

Kids' Games was conceived to address this problem for parents of children ages five to fifteen, though the upper age limit stretches considerably through skill variations and handicapping techniques. It is a collection of the most official rules to 129 of the best children's games, culled from the streets of New York City, the desert plains of Mozambique, the mountains of Malaysia . . . Some original games are also included.

With its comprehensive approach to defining the best games, this book is a "field guide" for learning to play, a resource that parents and children can rely upon to provide the most accurate rules available for a wide variety of games. The majority of the games require easily improvised equipment or none at all, and only a small percentage are dependent on special equipment, such as marbles, dominoes, cards, jacks, hopscotch heel, etc.

My greatest concern is that I provide people with a vehicle for play that draws on many types of skills. And I wanted to create a book that would be fun to read and use. Not "100 Things to Do on a Rainy Day" or "1001 Party Games." We played and tested every game and stripped out the boring ones in the process, no matter how great they sounded on paper.

On the premise that what the world needs is to have a lot more fun, *Kids' Games* contains games we feel are worth passing on to future generations.

I have selected most of the games for their familiarity and appeal. A few, such as NINUKI-RENJU and WARI, may be unfamiliar to some people because their names are taken from the Japanese and African equivalents, but both are classics known throughout the world. It did not seem fair or wise to rename any of the games.

The book is divided into two sections: Action Games and Nonaction Games, which was simply the easiest division to use. You can think of the sections as physical and mental games, outdoor and indoor games, whatever you wish. The four chapters constituting the Action Games section cover a wide variety of play, from CAPTURE THE FLAG to MUSICAL CHAIRS, from DODGEBALL to PAT-A-CAKE, from LEAPFROG to MARBLES. These are the games that provide some sort of physical activity, whether it be nonstop running or shooting a marble. The action games all involve some aspects of the player's manual dexterity and physical coordination.

By contrast, the Nonaction Games section includes more sedate challenges: word and number games, guessing games, card games, board games, pencil-and-paper games, and solitaire puzzles. These are the perfect games for after-dinner play, when you really don't want to run around any longer. These games challenge the minds, rather than the muscles, of the players. Some are games of chance; more are games of skill.

Each game description contains a note as to its origin, history, and cultural relationships, the rules of the game itself, and finally any variations of play, handicapping techniques, or suggestions for making or improvising the necessary gaming equipment.

I've enjoyed playing games all my life, and many of my favorites are included in the following pages. But, in researching this book, I discovered a realm of wonderful games from around the world that I never had a chance to play, because their rules were not available to me. I played "American" games, the games of my forefathers. I never even *heard* of WARI, and I'm sure it would have been one of the delights of my childhood.

So I am very happy to bring you all these games, but I'm a little sad, too. I think I missed out on a lot of fun. Please don't do the same.

—PHIL WISWELL
Cross River, 1986

SECTION I:

Action Games

CHAPTER ONE
Racing, Running, and Tagging Games

This group of games comprises some of the most active, physically exerting games in the book, because they all demand nearly constant movement from the players. You will find all kinds of physical exercise here, from games of tag to games of hiding and seeking, from dodging balls to kicking them, from relay races to jumping races.

These games and their many variations come from all over the world, most requiring no or little equipment. And all of them are quite easy to learn and remember, so they are excellent for groups of players young and old alike.

The games in this chapter may be taken seriously or lightly, strictly enforced or self-monitored, and none of the rules are hard and fast. You should feel free to experiment and expand on this group of games, tailoring the challenges to the type and amount of exercise you wish the games to provide.

RED ROVER

PLAYERS: *six or more*
LOCATION: *outdoors*
EQUIPMENT: *none*
SPECIAL SKILLS: *running, dodging*

RED ROVER is a game of aggression and physical power, and it is not recommended to anyone who can't take a scraped knee or elbow as part of the excitement. RED ROVER has its origins in Jockey Rover, a game made popular in Scotland during the late-nineteenth century.

There is no upper limit on the number of players, though fewer than six makes for a dull game. First, two team captains are chosen, then the captains pick members for their teams. It doesn't matter whether or not the teams divide evenly, so long as there is a fair distribution of strong players.

Each team creates a line facing the other from a distance of about twenty feet, forming a human chain by tightly holding hands. The captain of the team that did *not* get last pick of the players delivers the first challenge, which is chanted to the following rhyme:

> Red rover, red rover,
> Please send someone over.

Red rover, red rover,
Please send _____ over.

The captain fills in the blank with the name of a player from the opposing team. The player named in the rhyme must now rush the opposing human chain with the single object of breaking apart a pair of hands at any point in the chain, by any method short of really hurting another player. He may scream like a banshee, make horrible faces, and use all manner of psychological torture; in fact, this will give him a better chance for success.

The challenged player may not waste time or use more than the distance between the two teams in order to gain speed. If the player succeeds in breaking any link in the chain, he returns triumphantly to his own team along with his choice of the two players whose link was broken. If the player fails to break the chain, he remains and becomes part of it.

In RED ROVER, either you beat them or you join them.

By the way, the only rule governing success or failure is breaking a link in the chain. The team may end up in a tangled mess on the ground, but it captures the charging player if no link is broken.

The team captains alternately call a player from the other side by chanting the rhyme, and there is more strategy required by this than you may think. If you name a strong player from the other team, you hope to capture him, but you also risk losing a member of your chain to his powerful onslaught. And if you name a weak player, the odds are good you'll capture him, but then you will have a weak link in your chain. Much strategy also rests with the challenged player, who must decide whether to attack a strong or a weak link in the opposing chain. It is perfectly legal to call over the opposing team's captain. If a captain is captured, his old team elects a new one.

The game ends when one team has been reduced to a single player, and this is quite difficult. Most games tend to sway back and forth like a well-balanced round of Tug-of-War.

RED LION

PLAYERS: *six or more*
LOCATION: *outdoors*
EQUIPMENT: *none*
SPECIAL SKILLS: *running, dodging*

Although this game uses a chanting rhythm and has a similar title to RED ROVER, the two have nothing more in common—except that both are fantastic fun with a large crowd of players. It is such a popular game that it would be safe to claim that RED LION has been played on every street in America at one time or another.

You'll need at least five or six players to make RED LION work well, and a bigger group is even better. If there is little traffic on your street, a sidewalk makes a great boundary for the lion's den. I will describe the game as it is played in the street, but if that is not safe where you live, please improvise another location.

First, select one player to be the lion and send him into his den, the sidewalk. All other players remain in the street, a respectable distance from the sidewalk curb at the beginning of the game. The lion must remain in his den (on the sidewalk) until at least one player has challenged him to a chase. A player wishing to challenge the lion must touch the curb at any point within the boundaries (some people don't play with boundaries) and chant the rhyme:

Red lion, red lion,
Come out of your den.
Whoever you catch
Will be one of your men.

At any time after this taunting, the lion may leap from his den in pursuit of *any* prey—not just the taunting player. At this point, the other players run for the opposite sidewalk from the lion's den. Players who reach the sidewalk untagged are safe until the next round begins. But should the lion tag a player and shout, "Red lion!" three times before that player reaches safety, he may bring the captured prey back to his den. The prey now becomes the hunter and helps the lion chase down other players whenever the next taunting forces the lion to leap from his den.

The game continues in this manner until there is just one player left in the street. He is the winner.

CAPTURE THE FLAG

PLAYERS: *eight or more*
LOCATION: *outdoors*
EQUIPMENT: *two handkerchiefs*
SPECIAL SKILLS: *running, tagging, dodging*

When you have enough players for a game of touch football but you don't have a football, CAPTURE THE FLAG will fill an afternoon with the same kind of active, strategic, team-against-team competition. In fact, many players prefer this game to football because of its less complicated rules. Also, CAPTURE THE FLAG is not a male-oriented or male-dominated activity.

The origins of CAPTURE THE FLAG are obscure, but the game is obviously derived from warfare. Some scholars claim it to be an imitation of eighteenth-century territorial raids by England and Scotland across their common border, though I feel its origin is likely much older. In any case, CAPTURE THE FLAG was played in this country before it became the United States.

You can imagine much of how this game is played just from its title. Two teams try to capture each other's flag while protecting their own. First, players must agree upon the boundaries, which should be at least the size of a football field. Using chalk or white powder or imagination, divide the field of battle in the middle, one territory for each team, as shown in Diagram 1.1. At the rear of each territory, the team must hang or display its flag (any suitable piece of cloth the size of a handkerchief) in plain view. You may also wish to mark a ten-foot-square area near the flag as your team's jail. In any case, the jail is imaginary. One player from each team should be chosen as the jailer.

Another player should be elected general. It is the general's duty to plan the team strategy by sizing up his players and dividing them in half as raiding parties and lines of defense. The raiding parties are sent off to capture the opposing team's flag, while the lines of defense huddle around their own flag, nervously awaiting attack from the other team.

Diagram 1.1   CAPTURE THE FLAG

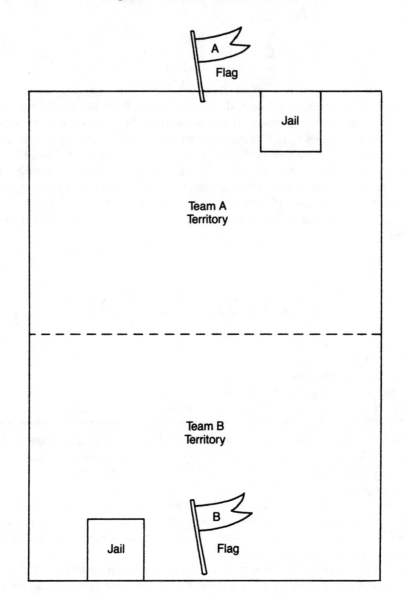

When the attack comes, well . . . anything goes! The defending team tries to repel and capture opposing-team members, whose sole object is to grab the flag and make it back to their own territory. The defense may capture a member of the raiding party by grabbing and holding on to some part of his body while shouting, "Caught! Caught! Caught!" The tagged player is then hauled off to jail.

Jailed members of the raiding party may only be freed by a teammate getting into the jail and shouting, "Freed! Freed! Freed!" before he can be caught. Hint: pick a jailer with good eyes. Freed players are given clear passage to their territory, where they will rejoin or re-form a raiding party. More than one raiding party acting as a decoy is a great tactic if you can spare players from your lines of defense.

The game continues until one team manages to bring the opposing team's flag into its territory.

KICK THE CAN, or TIN CAN TOMMY

PLAYERS: *five or more*
LOCATION: *outdoors*
EQUIPMENT: *one tin can*
SPECIAL SKILLS: *running, hiding, seeking*

This is the noisiest variation of Hide 'N' Seek known to youngsters, quite possibly the main reason for its worldwide popularity. References from cultures around the world show objects other than cans as the center of the game. But in the U.S.A. and Great Britain, the game just wouldn't be the same without that noisy tin can rattling on a sewer cover. Thus, its early popularity may be traced to the industrial revolution and the invention of canning processes.

You need as many players as you would for any decent game of Hide 'N' Seek, at least five in my opinion. The only equipment required is a tin can. Of course, almost anything nonbreakable will suffice: a plastic soda bottle, a block of wood, a catcher's mitt, etc. First, players agree who will begin as It (the seeker). It decides upon some central neighborhood spot, such as a sewer cover or sidewalk square, or It draws a similar shape with chalk. The can is placed in the center of the base.

Players now mill about, feinting this way and that, until one succeeds in kicking the can as far away from the base as possible. This player simultaneously announces the start of the round by shouting for all others to run and hide nearby, which they do. Meanwhile, It must chase down the can and return it to the center of the base using nothing except his feet. Additional time constraints may be placed on the seeker if players agree, such as counting to twenty-five before running after the can, or using a rubber ball as the can.

Once the can has been retrieved, It goes off in search of other players. When It spies someone in hiding, It shouts "_____, kick the can, one-two-three," filling in the blank with the hiding player's name. The hiding player is captured by this and must return to the base as a prisoner. However, while It is searching for other prisoners, free players may sneak up on the base and kick the can away, thereby freeing all prisoners to run and hide again. It must then return the can to the base with his feet before continuing the search.

The game is over when everyone is captured by It, or when everyone has gone home and you find yourself the only player remaining.

RING-O-LEVIO

PLAYERS: *four or more*
LOCATION: *outdoors*
EQUIPMENT: *none*
SPECIAL SKILLS: *running, chasing*

As my Italian friends explain it, RING-O-LEVIO is very popular with Italian-Americans, but it does not necessarily come from Italy. Rather, this game is simply the way people of Italian descent play tag in this country. There are hundreds of variations just like it. But since I wanted to include the simplest form of tag games in this chapter, I figured, Why not RING-O-LEVIO? There is something magical about its name.

Anyway, the game is best with a large group of players. This variation is meant to be played at dusk, when vision is down to a minimum and there is little else to do outside. First, select a player to be It and give him a flashlight. Establish some object as the base, such as a large tree, a car, a garage door—anything. It stands next to the base, closes his eyes, and gives all other players a chance to run and hide nearby within boundaries that all must agree on before the game begins.

It counts by ring-o-levios, like this: "One ring-o-levio, two ring-o-levio, three ring-o-levio, four ring-o-levio . . ." continuing to whatever number the group decided on for a head start. Now It turns on the flashlight and heads out to seek the other players, who are free to hide within or move about the boundaries of the game at will. A player is tagged when caught by the flashlight beam and identified by name. If It identifies the player incorrectly, the player remains free. Otherwise, the caught player is returned to the base.

While It is out searching for more players, they may sneak up and free the captured players by touching the base. Then It must recapture them.

The game usually continues until It gives up, unless you have an exceptionally talented It, because this game is really in favor of the hiding players.

In one variation of RING-O-LEVIO, the first player caught becomes the guard for the base for the remainder of the game. He remains at the base with captured players, attempting to tag free players before they can tag the base. If a free player tags the base without being tagged by the guard, all captured players are freed. If the free player is tagged by the guard, he is captured and must remain at the base with the others. This version of the game gives the advantage to It.

SARDINES

PLAYERS: *six or more*
LOCATION: *outdoors or in a large house*
EQUIPMENT: *none*
SPECIAL SKILLS: *hiding, seeking*

SARDINES is one of the cleverest variations of Hide 'N' Seek and tends to be as much fun for a group of adults as for children. Even more fun, given the right mix of players. No one takes credit for its invention, and I imagine it has been re-created countless times. Perhaps you saw them play it in the film *Pretty Baby*.

This is a game to be played with a small crowd of people, at least six or eight, and a dozen or more is even better. It is fine to play outdoors, provided you define a large and interesting hiding area, perhaps one that includes several small buildings. Indoors, with its many hiding places, is the usual locale, however.

One player is selected to hide first, and he is given a count of fifty or one hundred to disappear and find a good hiding place. After the time limit, all players disperse and begin searching. When a player finds the one hiding, he, too, enters the hiding place and waits for the others. One by one, a small crowd either ends up hiding in a small dark place or bursts forth in uncontrollable laughter as the last player wanders around alone.

There are no other rules to SARDINES. If you like to laugh, you'll love to play.

CATCHING STARS

PLAYERS: *six or more*
LOCATION: *outdoors*
EQUIPMENT: *none*
SPECIAL SKILLS: *running, tagging*

Children of African Pygmy tribes play a game associated with that culture's fascination with and tribute to the stars in the sky. It is a tagging game for a large group of players that requires neither equipment nor special skills. Notice the similarity between this game and our own American favorite RED LION.

First, select about one third or one fourth of the group to act as the catchers. The rest of the players are designated as stars. Draw two parallel lines about twenty feet apart, or play using the street curbs as boundaries if your street is a safe one. Side boundaries may be added or simply agreed upon by the players.

The stars stand on one of the lines and the catchers stand in the middle section. The catchers start the game or round by chanting the verse:

> "Star light, star bright,
> How many stars are out tonight?"

Upon hearing this, the stars shout, "More than you can catch!" and then try to run across the play area to the safety of the other line without being tagged. Any star tagged becomes a catcher for the next round. Thus the catchers can hope to grow in number with each round.

The game continues in this manner until there are no more stars to catch. At this point, new catchers are chosen and the game begins again. The last few players caught should be the new catchers unless the group feels otherwise.

PRISONER'S BASE

PLAYERS: *sixteen or more*
LOCATION: *outdoors*
EQUIPMENT: *chalk or powder*
SPECIAL SKILLS: *running, tagging*

This crazy variation on the theme of tag has been a favorite in Europe and England for hundreds of years at the very least. It is documented that Edward III, King of England, banned play of PRISONER'S BASE from the Westminster Palace grounds as it became such a popular nuisance. Edward III reigned from 1327 to 1377, so we can be sure this game is well over six hundred years old. Pass it on. And don't let your king ban it!

For the best effect, you'll need two teams of at least eight or nine players each, outfitted with different-colored shirts or armbands or something to distinguish members of the opposing teams from one another. One player should be selected as the captain of each team. Designate a large square area and mark it with chalk or powder if possible. Divide the square in half with a line down the middle, and draw a circle several feet in diameter in the center of this dividing line. Then draw a box in each corner of the square about four feet on a side. See Diagram 1.2.

Diagram 1.2   PRISONER'S BASE

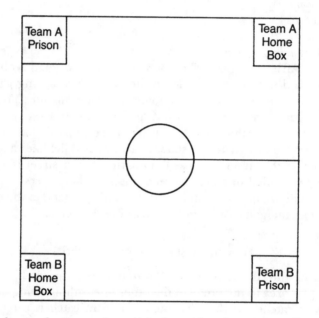

To begin play, each team gathers in its home box in a corner diagonally opposite from that of the other team. The remaining two boxes, in the other corners, are the prisons for the respective teams. Decide which team will go first.

The captain of that team usually sends out his best runner first. This player runs to the circle in the center of the field and shouts, "Chivy!" Don't ask me why. This signals the opposing team's captain to send out his best runner in an effort to tag the challenging player. Now the first captain can send out another runner trying to tag the one chasing his teammate, at which time the second captain may send out his next runner in pursuit.

Each player has just one member of the opposing team to tag and just one member of the opposing team chasing him as all four players head for their home bases. Tagged players are remanded to the other team's prison, where they must remain until freed by a tag from a team member in a subsequent round of play.

RED LIGHT! GREEN LIGHT!

PLAYERS: *four or more*
LOCATION: *outdoors*
EQUIPMENT: *none*
SPECIAL SKILLS: *running, stopping suddenly*

This game is native to the United States, and while no one recorded its early history, the game could not have evolved before the invention of the traffic light, sixty-odd years ago. In any case, to this day it is a very popular street game with children, requiring few skills and no equipment. It is another of the favorites from my early years.

You'll need at least four players to have fun with RED LIGHT! GREEN LIGHT! And the more the merrier. First, select one player as the light and have him stand with his back against a wall or a truck or a tree or anything convenient. The rest of the players should gather in a line about twenty feet away.

To begin play, the light turns around to face the wall or whatever, shouts, "Green light!" waits as many milliseconds as he dares, shouts, "One-two-three red light!" and whips around to face the other players. So long as the light is green and the light is not looking, the players are free to move toward him at top speed. But players must freeze in their tracks when the light turns red.

If the light detects even the slightest movement in a player, he may be sent back to the starting line. At his leisure, the light turns to face the wall again and the sequence continues. The first player to tag the light without being caught becomes the light for the next round.

Cheating is allowed, if you can get away with it. The light must see a player moving on a red light to send him back to the starting line.

CAT AND RAT

PLAYERS: *ten or more*
LOCATION: *outdoors*
EQUIPMENT: *none*
SPECIAL SKILLS: *running, chasing*

CAT AND RAT is a chase/tag game for a large group of children, especially good at those annual family get-togethers with all ages participating. The game should be played outdoors by at least ten people but no more than twenty, and it requires no equipment or special skills.

First, select one player for the rat and another for the cat. All other players should join hands and form a large circle. The cat stands outside the circle, the rat inside. When everyone is ready, the rat taunts the cat with the following: "I'm the rat! You can't catch me!" To this, the cat replies, "I'm the cat! We'll see, we'll see!" and the chase to tag the rat begins.

The players forming the circle are on the side of the rat (possibly for the first time in their lives!), and they must try to help him avoid the cat. One way they can do this is by making a nice high arch with their joined hands for the rat to pass through, but lowering the opening to slow down the cat in pursuit. Once any player in the circle of hands decides the cat has had enough, he calls out, "Open the gates!" and all players raise their hands high, leaving the rat on his own to evade the cat. Players must imagine a circular area around the circle of players as the boundaries, and the rat is not free to run outside this.

Once the rat is tagged, he and the cat become part of the circle of players and another cat and rat are selected for the next round.

STALKING GAME

PLAYERS: *eight or more*
LOCATION: *anywhere you have space*
EQUIPMENT: *two blindfolds*
SPECIAL SKILL: *none*

This amusing game comes to us from the African Bushmen of the Kalahari Desert, and imitates in childish fashion the serious purpose of the Kalahari hunter going after a springbok. Groups of African children have played this game for centuries. The only equipment you need to simulate their game is a pair of blindfolds or paper bags. The larger the group of players, the better the game and the longer you can make it last.

Choose two players to go first and have them stand in the middle of a large circle formed by the other players holding hands. One player is chosen to play the part of the springbok and the other is the hunter. Both are blindfolded (or you can use large paper bags) and spun around several times to disorient them. Then someone shouts the signal for the hunt to begin.

As quietly as they can, the two players begin moving around the circle, the springbok hoping to avoid the hunter and the hunter hoping to find and tag the springbok. The other players should remain as quiet as possible to give the hunter a better chance, though shouts of encouragement to both sides are within reason.

If the springbok succeeds in avoiding the hunter for a set amount of time, or whatever time the group sees fit, the springbok wins. In this case, the springbok selects the next hunter and remains in the game as the springbok for the next round. If the springbok is caught and the hunter wins, both players are replaced by a new pair.

LEAPFROG

PLAYERS: *two or more*
LOCATION: *outdoors*
EQUIPMENT: *none*
SPECIAL SKILLS: *running, jumping*

It may surprise you to know that the origin of the game of LEAPFROG goes back farther in time than it is possible to research. One popular myth holds that prehistoric men and women observed and mimicked the precocious activity of frogs, but don't believe it. I once saw some frogs observing children playing LEAPFROG, and they were confused by the whole thing.

Anyway, LEAPFROG has been startlingly popular with children in all cultures (except where there are no frogs, I suppose) since the Middle Ages, when it spread throughout Europe like plague. You will find references to LEAPFROG in paintings by Breughel, in Shakespeare's *Henry V,* and in many other famous works of art and literature. All children should experience this game. It is exciting and provides excellent, quit-when-you're-exhausted exercise.

Almost everyone I talk with has a different version of the game of LEAPFROG, but all are based on some general principles presented below. Please feel free to embellish the game in any manner you see fit. LEAPFROG is a kind of relay race for a large group of active kids, although it may also be played by two or three children as an active pastime. I will describe a competitive race between teams of leapfroggers.

First, form two or more teams of at least three players per team, and line them up at a starting point. Establish a finishing line according to general player agreement, involving, if you wish, a winding route. At the signal "GO!" the first player of each team takes a standing broad jump, then bends at the waist and grabs his ankles. This player is the first "back."

The next player takes a running start and vaults over the first player by placing the palms of both hands flat on the crouching player's back, spreading the legs, and leaping over. The jumping frog must land on both feet without falling over, then bend down and take hold of his ankles, becoming the lead "back." Now there are two backs, and the third player must vault over both in succession without hesitating or knocking over the "backs." He must jump the first, landing on his feet, and continue by jumping the second.

If a jumping frog does *not* land on his two feet, or if he knocks over any "backs" in the chain, he must return to the end of his team's line. In this manner, a poor jump does not advance the position of the team.

When the last member of a team has successfully jumped the chain of his teammates, the last player in the chain stands up and becomes the next jumping frog. If he does not succeed in leaping the entire chain, he must return to the back end of the chain and try again until he does.

There are no rules governing when the next frog may begin jumping. And since the object is to be the fastest chain of frogs to the finish line, it is to your advantage to start leaping before the last leaper has finished his jumps. Of course, this means you'll have to return and try again if either he or you makes a mistake. Try not to crash into the back of the last leaper. And when you finish your leap, grab your ankles and bend quickly, because the next leaping frog may be right on your tail!

INDIAN KICKBALL

PLAYERS: *six or more*
LOCATION: *outdoors*
EQUIPMENT: *two softballs*
SPECIAL SKILLS: *running, kicking*

The game of KICKBALL, thousands of years old, originates with the Tarahumara Indians of Mexico, a tribe whose name means "foot runners" and whose members play KICKBALL as much more than a race game of endurance and skill. What chess means to Russian children, KICKBALL means to the children of the Tarahumara, who begin training as runners from early childhood in hopes of one day running on the winning team.

This yearly race run by the Tarahumara is performed with great celebration among the village spectators who line the routes taken by the runners, gambling and drinking as if it were the Kentucky Derby. It is a very difficult race, covering twenty to thirty miles of rocky terrain; it is also a very unusual race in that it is not run alone. Instead, three to six runners constitute a team, and the team cooperates to move its ball across the finish line first, using only their feet.

In the United States, this game is still played by the Hopi Indians as a ritual preceded by prayer. This is not as silly as you may think: the Hopi use a *stone* ball and no shoes on their feet. The ball used by the Tarahumara is carved from the root of a tree. They don't use shoes either.

You will need at least two teams of three to six members per team to play KICKBALL. Each team uses one ball, which need not be a stone or carved from the root of a tree. Still, the ball should be one that cannot be kicked great distances with ease. Use an old softball or make a ball yourself. Make a grapefruit-sized ball of aluminum foil and wrap it in strips of leather or rubber. And let everyone wear shoes!

The teams should agree upon a course for the race, walking it first if necessary, to establish the guidelines. The course should be between a hundred yards and two or more miles long, with definite start and finish lines. Line up the team members at the starting line and signal the beginning of the race. One runner from each team kicks or pushes his team's ball forward, then moves out of the way for another team member, and so forth. No particular order need be kept, so long as the same player doesn't kick or push the ball twice in a row. Each team must police itself on this point, but it becomes a natural part of the challenge after a while.

The ball may not be touched with any part of a runner's body except the foot. The only other rule concerns winning: the first team over the finish line, of course.

SPOON RACING

PLAYERS: *eight or more*
LOCATION: *outdoors*
EQUIPMENT: *two spoons, two teacups, two pails of water*
SPECIAL SKILL: *balance*

This delightful gem is a relay race that tests and builds nerve, coordination, and surefootedness. There are very few playrooms that can withstand the results of this game, so please play outside.

Form as many teams as you need for a relay race, with at least four players per team. Line up each team at a starting point and give the first player in each line a large serving spoon. (You can use a team of adults, but they must be handicapped by using a teaspoon.) Place a pail or pan full of water at the head of each line.

About twenty-five feet away, place a teacup for each team on a level surface, either raised or on the ground, the latter making the game more difficult.

At the word "GO!" the first team member scoops up as much water as his spoon will hold and heads for the teacups. A player may return for more water at any point along the way, but he must arrive at his team's teacup with at least *some* contribution on his spoon, which is emptied into the cup. The player then runs back to his team as fast as he can, dropping the spoon in the pail of water for the next team member.

The race continues until one team has filled its teacup and is declared the winner. It is a wise idea to use an impartial judge for SPOON RACING.

NEWSPAPER RACE

PLAYERS: *eight or more*
LOCATION: *anywhere you have space*
EQUIPMENT: *a newspaper*
SPECIAL SKILL: *none*

This strange kind of relay race likely has thousands of origins, but I like to think it must have been devised by a father in charge of a dozen children with nothing in his possession but a newspaper. He would, of course, gladly have given up that newspaper and the rest of his worldly goods if only the children would play nicely and stop giving him so much trouble.

In any case, this is a very amusing race game, guaranteed to break the age barrier and a wonderful activity for those big family get-togethers. Incidentally, the windier the day the more fun and challenging NEWSPAPER RACE becomes.

First, divide into teams with enough members per team for a decent relay race, say at least four per team. Create a starting line and have each team form a line behind it. Give the first player in line two full sheets of newspaper. Establish a finishing line about twenty-five yards away, then give the signal to begin.

The object is for each player to race to the finishing line and back to his team, with the following single condition: he must not allow any part of his body (or his shoes) to touch the ground. If it does, he must return to the starting line and begin his turn again. It is legal to drag the newspaper with your foot, though you risk tearing it, or to let the wind lift the papers as you move, though that risks losing your precious stepping stones. Should a player become separated from one of his sheets of paper, he may return to the starting line and begin again, using a new sheet.

Keep a good supply of newspaper on hand, because rematches are fairly standard with this race.

FEATHER RACING

PLAYERS: *six or more*
LOCATION: *anywhere you have space*
EQUIPMENT: *two feathers, two paper plates*
SPECIAL SKILL: *balance*

The simple and quite hilarious game of FEATHER RACING seems to have an American heritage, but it is very difficult to pin down. For fun, let's assume the game was devised a hundred years ago, somewhere in the farm belt, where feathers are easier to come by than fun!

FEATHER RACING is a relay race that is best played with several teams of at least three or four players per team. You may play in the backyard, but a long room will do nicely too. First, create starting and finishing lines. The length of the race is up to you and the players; you should consider ages and skill levels. If necessary, you may handicap a team of older, more skillful players by extending their finishing line farther than the others'.

Line up the teams at the starting line and give the first player of each team a paper plate on which a small feather sits. At the signal "GO!" players race to the finish line and back to the starting line as fast as they can without dropping the feather. No player may touch the feather in any way during the race. If a feather falls or is blown off a plate, that player must pick it up and return to the starting line to begin his relay again.

As you can imagine, FEATHER RACING is not a test of speed. Rather, it is a test of coordination, determination, and how much you know about the winds in your backyard. Although you may race indoors, it's just not quite as good without the unknown factor of wind.

HARVEST RACE

PLAYERS: *twelve—six per team*
LOCATION: *outdoors*
EQUIPMENT: *see below*
SPECIAL SKILL: *none*

This relay-race game is very popular with children in China, where great value is placed upon cooperation in games as in everyday life. There is nothing political about the game—you can play whether you favor democracy or communism. The point is that HARVEST RACE is an exciting relay race with a theme that appeals to children the world over.

The game is played with teams of exactly six members per team, but you can modify the game to suit the number of players. The idea is that each player has a different task to perform in the raising of imaginary crops. For fewer players, cut down the number of tasks.

Also, feel free to use imaginary items if necessary, but children really like using the real hoe, watering can, et cetera. It's up to you.

Set up a starting line about fifty yards away from a "garden," a patch of ground the players can dig in. If you are playing with six-player teams, each team needs the following items: a hoe, some plastic flowers, a watering can, a bucket of fertilizer, a spray can, and a basket. Each team's items are placed in a pile in the garden.

Each team decides who will have which task; then they line themselves up. On the signal "GO!" the first player of each team runs to the garden, picks up the hoe, hoes three holes in the ground, drops the hoe in the pile, and races back to tag the next team member. This second player must run to the garden, plant three plastic flowers in the holes and cover the holes with dirt, then return to the starting line. The third player waters the flowers; the fourth sprinkles fertilizer on them; the fifth sprays the leaves for bugs, and the last player picks the flowers, places them in the basket, and races back. Sometimes each team is also equipped with a bicycle or a tricycle that the last player must use to "pedal his crops" back to the team.

The first team to harvest its crop of three flowers wins.

THE PUZZLE HUNT

PLAYERS: *any number*
LOCATION: *anywhere*
EQUIPMENT: *picture postcards*
SPECIAL SKILL: *none*

Also known as The Jigsaw Game, THE PUZZLE HUNT is a wonderful icebreaker for any gathering of children. Though it takes a bit of preparation, it is one of the easiest party games to explain, and any number of players are accommodated. It requires no skill except for good eyesight.

To get ready for the game, you must prepare a small, simple jigsaw puzzle for each player. You may use postcards, advertisements, magazine covers, or whatever, but make sure each player's is different enough from the others to be highly recognizable. Cut the postcards or whatever you're using into at least four jagged pieces, making a crude jigsaw puzzle from each. Then hide all but one piece of each puzzle somewhere in the same large room. Make sure you do this before the get-together begins, so that no player sees where you're hiding the pieces.

Once all the players are assembled, give each one of the remaining pieces. Instruct the children to locate the other pieces of their puzzles. The first player to find all his pieces and put them together is the winner.

This game can be adapted for any age group by making the jigsaw puzzles more difficult—either more pieces or more difficult to recognize and put back together.

THE SPIDER'S WEB

PLAYERS: *any number*
LOCATION: *anywhere*
EQUIPMENT: *string, prizes*
SPECIAL SKILL: *none*

This game came to me through a large family who used to live across the street. On holidays and special occasions, the parents would prepare this "untangling" race to their children's delight every time. It is an elegant idea that has a bonus: you won't hear from the children for a long while, once they begin. THE SPIDER'S WEB is simple enough for a five-year-old and engaging enough to hold the attention of the teenage crowd.

Here's how it works. First, you'll need a small gift or edible treat for each player, plus a lot of string. Fasten a string to each of the gifts, hide them in various places, then wind each string around furniture, stairway banisters, other strings, and whatever you can find that will make a nicely tangled mess. You can handicap the older players by making their trails more difficult to untangle. Show each player to the free end of a piece of string.

The winner is the first player to retrieve his gift by completely untangling his string and winding it into a tidy ball.

If you have a lot of trees and open shrubbery, the game is even better played outside. In that case, use much longer strings that send players all over the playing area.

CHAPTER TWO
Coordination Games

The category of "Coordination Games" is my invention, but it does seem to comprise a set of games with similar characteristics. All the games in this category require some type of physical coordination, such as dexterity of the hands, arms, feet, and legs, without requiring much physical exertion.

I take wide license with the selection of games for this chapter, which range from the quiet of TIDDLYWINKS and JACKS to the riotous STORK FIGHTS and INDIAN WRESTLING. However, I feel that variety is important, and the wider the variety the better the games.

About half the games in this chapter are played traditionally by American schoolchildren, and the other half come from all over the world. Don't be put off by a strange-sounding title—you may rename the games if you wish.

The range of challenges to be found below encompasses many skills of manual dexterity and physical coordination, providing discipline for both body and mind. By the way, you may use the game JAN-KEM-PO, found below, as a method for determining who goes first in other games.

JAN-KEM-PO

PLAYERS: *any number*
LOCATION: *anywhere*
EQUIPMENT: *none*
SPECIAL SKILL: *reaction timing*

Japanese children play a game called JAN-KEM-PO with their fingers, the origin of the Western game of Rock-Paper-Scissors. In this country, Rock-Paper-Scissors is most often played to choose a player to go first in some other game. In Japan, JAN-KEM-PO is played as a game all by itself. Any number can play, and there is no equipment needed.

JAN-KEM-PO is a blend of agility, speed, skill, and a little luck. It also helps if you memorize the hand signals and what they mean. Holding out a fist represents a rock. Holding out the hand palm down with fingers spread represents a piece of paper. Holding out index and middle finger in a V shape represents a pair of scissors.

The simple circular rule governing the game goes like this: rock breaks scissors, scissors cut paper, and paper covers rock. Learn this rule well.

To play the game JAN-KEM-PO, select one player to go first. This player should stand in full sight of the others, make a fist with his right hand, and stroke the fist along his left arm three times, saying the words JAN-KEM-PO each time. On the last stroke, the player shoots out his hand held in one of the three positions of rock, paper, or scissors.

All other players should react immediately by shooting their hands out in one of the positions, attempting to choose the position that will beat the one shown by the chosen player. The first player to "beat" the chosen player wins. Remember: rock beats scissors, scissors beat paper, and paper beats rock.

When another player has beaten the first player twice, he becomes the leader for the next round.

TIDDLYWINKS

PLAYERS: *two to four*
LOCATION: *any flat surface*
EQUIPMENT: *plastic disks, small cup*
SPECIAL SKILL: *none*

TIDDLYWINKS is such a silly-sounding game that many players will never try it. This is a mistake, because TIDDLYWINKS is a challenging game of manual dexterity and coordination that is unlike any other game. Nothing else even comes close to imitating the type of skill and level of concentration required by TIDDLYWINKS.

Usually the game is played by two competing players or just one player practicing for a big match, but the game will accommodate more than two. I'd say the limit is five players, and even then the playing field would get very crowded.

Some players prefer the floor as a playing field, but a square or round table is more comfortable and also provides definite boundaries. In any case, the surface should be smooth and covered with a flat piece of felt or a thick cloth. The ideal playing surface is a pool table, but many players become tempted to play pool, rather than TIDDLYWINKS, so stick to a table covered with felt or cloth.

Place the cup in the center of the table. You may decide on your own size for the cup, but regulations generally place the cup at one and a half inches in diameter by one to two inches high. These are easily fashioned from paper cups, so you might experiment with the size by making several.

Each player must have a supply of winks—which are smooth, flat plastic disks about the size of a nickel—and a shooter, a plastic disk the size of a quarter. Each player should use winks of a unique color to distinguish them from those of the opponents. Many people go out and buy a set of TIDDLYWINKS when, sitting unused in some board game on the top shelf of the closet, is a bag of suitable winks from some boring old board game. Suit yourself, but I'd improvise.

Each player places one of his winks on the edge of the table in line with those of the other players and takes a single shot at the cup. The player who comes closest goes first, and the order of play is determined. Players should arrange themselves so that play will proceed clockwise around the table. A round table is perfect, because it allows all players to easily line up their winks at equal distance from the cup at the beginning of the game. See Diagram 2.1 for a sample opening position.

There is no limit on the number of winks each player may use, so long as everyone has the same number. Four or five each will do.

In turn, a player uses his shooter (the larger plastic disk) to cause one of his own winks to jump in the direction of the cup. This is done by applying pressure to one

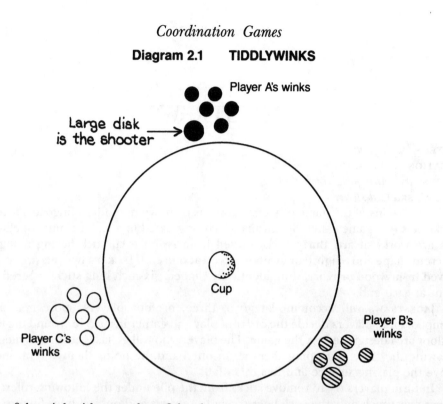

Diagram 2.1   TIDDLYWINKS

edge of the wink with one edge of the shooter and gradually drawing the shooter off the wink.

If a player's shot goes into the cup, it remains there and the player gets another shot with one of his remaining winks. Once several turns have passed, players decide whether to advance previously shot winks closer to the cup or to enter new winks from the border of the table. This is always the choice of the individual player.

A wink that becomes partially covered by another wink may not be shot until the covering wink has been shot off of it. If a wink goes off the table, it is returned to a spot on the edge near where it went out of bounds.

The first player to shoot all of his winks into the cup is the winner.

VARIATIONS

There are thousands of variations on the game of TIDDLYWINKS; many of these are based on sports games such as tennis, golf, or even badminton, shooting a wink back and forth across a line and within the boundaries of a rectangular court. You can probably devise your own variations rather easily just by applying the rules of some sport you know, so I won't bother listing variations here. Just one idea: make up a TIDDLYWINKS nine-hole golf course that covers an entire room, complete with sand and water traps and other hazards.

JACKSTRAWS

PLAYERS: *two to four*
LOCATION: *any level space*
EQUIPMENT: *thirty jackstraws*
SPECIAL SKILL: *dexterity*

The origins of the game of JACKSTRAWS, also known in modern lingo as Pick-Up-Sticks, lies in a game called Spellicans which originated in ancient China. Spellicans sets are works of art, thirty sticks carved from ivory, each stick having a slightly different shape and a figure or symbol carved at one end. JACKSTRAWS sets are usually carved from wood or ivory, thin, identically shaped, six-inch long sticks tapered to a point at each end.

JACKSTRAWS will accommodate two, three, or four players; more gets a bit cramped. First, players decide the order of play and gather in a circle around the table or floor area designated for the game. The player who will go last gets the privilege of throwing the sticks. Grasping them all in one hand, he holds them several inches above the playing surface and lets them fall.

In turn, players try to remove sticks from the pile under the following rules: 1) a player may touch only the stick he is trying to retrieve and only with his fingers, and 2) in retrieving it from the tangled pile he may not disturb the position of any other stick.

A successfully retrieved jackstraw entitles the player to keep it and try for another on the same turn. If a player makes a mistake, he leaves the stick he was trying to retrieve, and play passes to the next player. The game ends when there are no more jackstraws available. Then each player counts the jackstraws he retrieved during the game, and the player with the greatest number is declared the winner.

It is very easy to make a set of jackstraws. Get some three-foot-long wooden dowels—thin ones, about one-eighth of an inch in diameter—and cut them into six-and-one-half-inch lengths. Then taper the ends to a point with a small-size pencil sharpener and/or sandpaper. Paint or varnish is optional.

FIVESTONES, or KNUCKLEBONES

PLAYERS: *two to four*
LOCATION: *any smooth, level area*
EQUIPMENT: *five pebbles*
SPECIAL SKILL: *dexterity*

The modern game of JACKS, or JACKSTONES, as it is sometimes called, was derived from a primitive concept of tossing and catching small objects in increasingly more difficult patterns using both front and back of the throwing hand. In ancient Greece and throughout Asia Minor, the game was known by many names, among them FIVESTONES and KNUCKLEBONES. These names arose due to the use of small stones and the knucklebones of sheep as playing pieces.

You may play these games using five pebbles or five modern jacks. Or you can improvise. I've played using Chicklets, dried baked beans, dice, and the little wooden cubes from a Diplomacy board game. In this section, playing pieces will be referred to as stones.

A game of FIVESTONES is actually a lot of little games strung together, an increasingly more difficult set of challenges. The object is to be the first player to complete the set. The paragraphs that follow describe one such series, and there are many more challenges you may incorporate. Play begins with the easier challenges and progresses through the difficult ones. If a player succeeds on any challenge, he may attempt the next one on the same turn.

To start any game of FIVESTONES, all players hold their five stones in the palm of one hand, toss them into the air, and catch as many as possible on the *back* of the same hand. The player catching the most stones in this manner goes first. Throw again for a tie.

Jockey, or **Basic Throw:** The player holds the five stones in the palm of one hand, tosses them into the air, and attempts to catch them all on the back of his hand. If all are caught, they are retossed, from the back of the hand, and the player attempts to catch them all in his palm. If all are caught, the player continues to the next challenge. Otherwise, play passes to the next player.

Ones: The player holds the five stones in the palm of one hand and scatters them onto the playing surface. He then picks up the stone of his choice, tosses it into the air, grabs one of the remaining four stones, and catches the tossed stone with the same hand. If he succeeds, the player transfers one of the two caught stones to his other hand, tosses the remaining one into the air, grabs another stone from the playing surface, and catches the tossed stone. The player continues in this manner until all four stones have been picked up successfully. If he succeeds, he continues to the next challenge. Otherwise, play passes.

Twos: This is the same as **Ones,** except the player attempts to pick up two stones at a time rather than one. If he succeeds in picking up both pairs of stones, he continues to the next challenge.

Threes: This is the same as **Twos,** except the player attempts to pick up three stones on the first toss and one on the second. If he succeeds, he continues to the next challenge.

Fours: This is the same as **Threes,** except the player attempts to pick up all four stones on the first toss. If he succeeds, he continues to the next challenge.

Pecks: This game begins with the **Jockey** throw. If successful, he continues to the next challenge, **Bushels.** If no stones are caught in the palm, his turn ends and he must try again on his next turn. If two or more stones are caught in the palm, the player must work one of them toward the end of his hand so that he may hold it between two fingertips. Then the player closes his palm on the others, tosses the stone between his fingertips into the air, grabs one stone from the playing surface, and catches the tossed stone. This must be repeated until the player has picked up all the stones he missed on the original throw.

Bushels: This game also begins with the **Jockey** throw. If successful, a player continues to the next challenge, **Claws.** If no stones are caught in the palm, his turn ends. If he catches one or more stones in the palm, he must toss them into the air, grab one stone from the playing surface, and catch all the falling stones. This must be repeated until the player has picked up all the stones he missed on the original throw.

Claws: The player begins with the **Jockey** throw. If successful, the player continues to **Ones Under the Arch.** If no stones are caught on the back of the hand, his turn ends. If one or more stones are caught on the back of the hand, they must remain there while the player picks up all the others between the fingers of his throwing hand, no more than one stone between any two fingers. Then the stone or stones on the back of his hand must be tossed into the air and caught in the palm. Finally the stones held between the fingers are transferred into the palm.

Ones Under the Arch: The player scatters the five stones onto the playing surface, then makes an arch nearby with the thumb and forefinger of the nonthrowing hand. The player picks up the stone of his choice, tosses it into the air, knocks another stone through the arch, and catches the tossed stone. This is repeated until all four stones have been knocked through the arch.

Twos Under the Arch: This is the same as the previous game except the player knocks two stones at a time through the arch.

Threes Under the Arch: This is the same as the previous game except the player knocks three stones through the arch on the first toss and one through the arch on the second.

Fours Under the Arch: This is the same as the previous game except the player knocks all four stones through the arch on the first toss.

Stables: The player scatters the five stones onto the playing surface, then makes a "stable" with four doors by touching the fingers and thumb of the nonthrowing hand onto the playing surface. The player selects the stone of his choice, tosses it into the air, knocks any stone through one of the stable doors (between a pair of fingers), and catches the tossed stone. This is repeated until each door has received one stone.

Toad in the Hole: The player scatters the five stones onto the playing surface, then makes a "hole" by touching the tips of the thumb and forefinger together on the nonthrowing hand. The hole is placed flat on the surface. The player selects the stone of his choice, tosses it into the air, grabs any stone from the playing surface, drops it into the hole, and catches the tossed stone. This is repeated until all four "toads" are in the hole.

JACKS

PLAYERS: *two to four*
LOCATION: *any smooth, level area*
EQUIPMENT: *jacks, small rubber ball*
SPECIAL SKILL: *dexterity*

The basic rules to FIVESTONES and the modern JACKS games are quite similar, since JACKS is just an extension of the earlier game, though the addition of the bouncing ball adds variation. I will describe some of the more commonly played games.

JACKS may be played using pebbles as in olden times or using a modern set of jacks. It may also be played with or without a ball. The games using the ball and a modern set of jacks are generally easier for young children. Playing without the ball or with pebbles for pieces requires more skill.

The following sequence of challenges illustrates one modern game of JACKS using a set of jacks (usually six or ten per player, depending on their skill) and a rubber ball. You may include any of these within your series, and should feel free to add other variations.

Baby Game: The player scatters the jacks on the playing surface, then tosses the ball into the air, picks up one jack, using the same hand, while the ball bounces once, then catches the ball before it bounces a second time. The jack is then transferred to the nonthrowing hand, and the player tries for another jack. This is repeated until all six or ten jacks have been retrieved.

Twos, Threes, Fours, etc.: These games, taken in sequence, are played the same as the **Baby Game,** except the jacks must be retrieved two at a time, three at a time, four at a time, and so forth.

Downs and Ups: The player holds the ball and jacks in the throwing hand, tosses the ball, scatters the jacks, and catches the ball after one bounce. The player then tosses the ball again, picks up all the jacks at once, and catches the ball after one bounce.

Eggs in the Basket: The player scatters the jacks, tosses the ball, picks up one jack, transfers it to the nonthrowing hand, and catches the ball after one bounce. When all the "eggs" are in the "basket," the same game is played again, this time picking up two eggs at a time. Then three at a time, four at a time, and so forth.

Crack the Eggs: The player scatters the jacks, tosses the ball, picks up one jack, taps it against the playing surface (cracking the egg), and catches the ball. The cracked egg is then transferred to the nonthrowing hand and the player continues cracking the remaining eggs. Again, when all eggs are in the nonthrowing hand, they are scattered and picked up and cracked two at a time, three at a time, four at a time, and so forth.

Pigs in the Pen: The player scatters the jacks and cups his nonthrowing hand near them on the playing surface, forming a completely enclosed "pen." The player tosses the ball, simultaneously opens the pen by lifting his thumb, and shoves a jack into it with the throwing hand, then catches the ball after one bounce. This is repeated until all the pigs are safely in the pen. As with the previous two games, the jacks are then scattered again and retrieved two at a time, three at a time, and so forth.

Pigs over the Fence: The player scatters the jacks and places his nonthrowing hand near them with four fingers stacked as the "fence." The player tosses the ball, grabs one of the jacks, places it on the other side of the fence, and catches the ball after one bounce. Again, when this challenge is complete, the jacks are scattered and retrieved in units of two, three, four, five, and six.

MARBLES

PLAYERS: *six or fewer*
LOCATION: *smooth, packed dirt*
EQUIPMENT: *marbles*
SPECIAL SKILL: *aiming*

Some crude version of the game of MARBLES is likely as old as cavemen and small round rocks, the flat floor of a well-worn cave being the ideal terrain for shooting marbles. There are many references to games played with marble-sized objects in the literature of nearly every civilization, dating back to ancient Egypt and Rome thousands of years ago. It is a timeworn and honored tradition among the world's children to make and collect and shoot these little balls off their thumbs at various targets, and the game has changed little over the years. In fact, marbles themselves have changed more than the game variations, beginning as rounded-off rocks and progressing through true carved marble to baked clay and glass and hollow steel.

There are so many different games you can play with a set of marbles that many books have been written on the subject. I will present several popular ones below, but if you're really interested, check your library for other resources.

Bombardier: This is one of the simplest MARBLES variations, requiring the least amount of skill and thus well suited for young players. Draw a circle in the dirt twelve inches in diameter, and have each player contribute two or three marbles to a group placed in the center of the circle. This group is the target. In turn, each player drops a marble from about eighteen inches directly over the group, hoping to knock marbles outside the circle, because they become the property of the current player. Play continues until there are no more target marbles within the circle.

The Ring Game: This variation, one of the most popular of the modern MARBLES games, is usually played by just two. First, dig a circle in the dirt between three and six feet in diameter, depending on the skill of the players. Use a smaller circle for younger players. This circle should be dug like a trench about a half inch wide and a half inch deep, to prevent the marbles from rolling away. In the center of the circle dig thirteen small impressions in the dirt as shown in Diagram 2.2. Place a marble in each of these impressions, forming a cross in the center of the circle.

Diagram 2.2   MARBLES: THE RING GAME

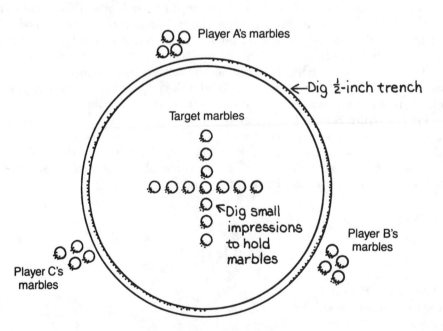

When shooting marbles, certain rules must be followed: 1) at least one knuckle of the shooting hand must rest on the ground and may not move until the marble has left the hand. 2) The marble must be flicked out with the thumb only.

In turn, players kneel at any point outside the circle and "knuckle down," with the marble held between forefinger and thumb. The players shoot their marbles alternately at the target marbles in the center of the ring. If a player knocks a marble outside the ring, his turn continues from the exact spot where his shooter comes to rest, so long as the shooter remains within the ring. Any marble knocked outside the ring becomes the property of the shooter.

A player's turn ends when he fails to knock a marble out of the ring. In this case, he retrieves his shooter and waits for his next turn, which he may take from any point on the perimeter of the circle. The game continues until there are no more marbles. The winner is the player who ends up with the greatest number of marbles.

Through the Arches: This is a popular MARBLES target game for which you'll need to make a target. The easiest method is to cut arches in a cardboard box as shown in Diagram 2.3. The five arches should decrease in size to the center arch, which should be about one inch wide. Number each arch with a target value of your choice. I suggest 3-5-10-5-3, giving more points to the more difficult shots.

Diagram 2.3   MARBLES: THROUGH THE ARCHES

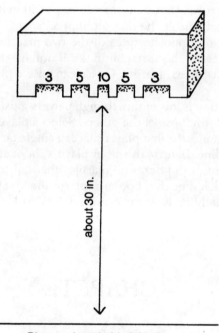

Players shoot behind this line

Establish a shooting line about thirty inches away on a smooth, flat surface. In turn, each player knuckles down and shoots all his marbles (any number you like) at the target and scores the points. Play continues to an agreed-upon winning total or an agreed-upon number of rounds. The player with the highest score is the winner.

Capture: This is a good MARBLES game for a group of four or more players. First, draw a shooting line about twenty inches long, and decide on an order of play. The first player shoots his marble anywhere onto the field. The next player shoots a marble at the first player's. If he hits it, he retrieves both marbles. If he misses, he leaves both. The third player then shoots, and so forth, with more and more marbles accumulating on the field, until some of them are won and removed from play. The game ends when all the marbles have been won, and the winner obviously is the player with the greatest number.

Against the Wall: This delightful variation of **Capture** is for any number of players, each shooting just a single marble. Establish a shooting line about ten feet away from a wall, and an order of play. The first player shoots his marble against the wall and lets it remain where it lies. In turn, each player shoots his marble against the wall. If a player hits another marble on the rebound off the wall, he claims all marbles on the ground. If not, he leaves the marble where it lies.

In case no player's marble has hit another player's marble legitimately on this first round, a second is begun. However, on this round the players shoot from the positions of their marbles, much closer to their intended targets.

Spangy: This variation is designed for five players, but you could improvise otherwise. Draw a square one foot by one foot in the dirt about ten feet away from a shooting line as shown in Diagram 2.4, and have each player place a marble on one of the five locations in the diagram. In turn, players shoot from behind the line, aiming to knock a target marble out of the square.

If a marble is knocked outside the square, it becomes the property of the shooter, who then gets another turn. Also, if his marble stops within the span of his thumb and forefinger from a target marble, he may attempt a "span." To do this, he places his thumb and forefinger on opposite sides of the two marbles and attempts to knock them together. If successful, his turn continues. If not, his turn ends, and his shooter remains in the square as an extra target. On a clean miss, a player retrieves his shooter after his turn.

Alleys: This variation is lots of fun, though players must constantly risk their own marbles attempting to win those of the others. Select a player to go first and an order of play. To begin the game, the first player places a single target marble about ten feet away from a shooting line. In turn, the other players shoot at this target from the line. The first player continues to pocket all marbles that fail to hit the target until one meets the mark, at which time the shooter replaces the first player as collector of bad shots. This game usually ends when no one wants to lose any more marbles. Of course, you could always agree to give them back after the game.

CHAPETE

PLAYERS: *three to six*
LOCATION: *outdoors*
EQUIPMENT: *small leather ball or beanbag*
SPECIAL SKILLS: *hopping, kicking, balancing*

CHAPETE is a popular game that has been played among Mexican and Central and South American teenagers and young adults for centuries. Only recently has it begun to gain broad popularity in the United States, possibly due to trends in American fitness. You see, CHAPETE is a very active and athletic game, although you don't actually move anywhere. It's kind of like juggling or running in place.

Also, a company began marketing the game under the name of Hacky Sack several years ago. Of course, the Hacky Sack consists of the ball and a small sheet of rules. You can make your own "ball" by sewing something pliable and of medium

Diagram 2.4   MARBLES: SPANGY

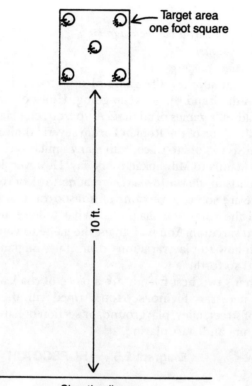

Target area
one foot square

10 ft.

Shooting line

weight inside a piece of leather or thick cloth. You could fill it with beans or rice or sand or some other easily accessible substance.

CHAPETE may be played by any number of players, but you should limit a group to between four and eight very coordinated players. The object of the game is as simple as they come: to keep a small beanbag-like ball aloft. Believe me, this sounds a lot easier than it is.

The only rule to CHAPETE is that no player may touch the ball with any part of his body above the waist. A player may kick the ball with foot, knee, or thigh, either to another player or to himself.

To play, form a circle with the other players, then launch the ball into play. Remember, this is a cooperative game, so the only way to score is to keep the ball aloft. Score your group on the number of kicks the ball receives before it hits the ground.

And try not to kick the other players by mistake!

HOPSCOTCH

PLAYERS: *two to four*
LOCATION: *anywhere you may draw the diagram*
EQUIPMENT: *chalk, shoe heel*
SPECIAL SKILLS: *aiming, jumping*

How old do you suppose the game of HOPSCOTCH is? A hundred years? Five hundred years? A thousand years? Keep going! HOPSCOTCH is one of the oldest and most popular children's games of all time. A HOPSCOTCH diagram can still be seen as it was etched into the floor of the Roman Forum several thousand years ago. The exact origin of the game is too old to trace, with many similar variations still actively played from Moscow to Manila to Milwaukee every day. However, it is certain that the game spread to many parts of the world via the great network of roads built by the Romans.

Today, there are so many versions of HOPSCOTCH that books have been written just to detail all the rules and diagrams. What follows are the rules to the most general, standard variation. You may adapt the game to your local rules or go to the library and learn how to play variations from Italy, England, France, Germany, the Netherlands, and so forth.

A hopscotcher's two best friends are a piece of chalk and an old shoe heel, the only equipment necessary for HOPSCOTCH. Armed with these two items, you simply find a safe area of street, alley, playground, or section of hard-packed dirt on which to draw your diagram, and start playing.

Diagram 2.5   HOPSCOTCH

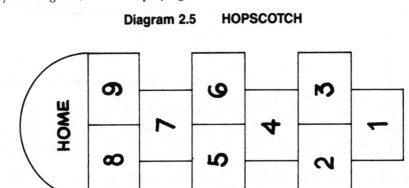

Diagram 2.5 shows one of the most common HOPSCOTCH outlines. Draw this diagram (or your own variation) on the paved surface. Diagram 2.6 shows a variation of the same outline, just using different shapes for the 4, 5, 6, and 7 spaces. I asked three friends to each draw the HOPSCOTCH diagrams they remembered playing when growing up in their respective native countries of Haiti, Argentina, and China. Interestingly, all three drew Diagram 2.7, in which you hop through most of the diagram on one foot.

You may feel free to experiment with the dimensions of each box in any of these diagrams or draw your own, sizing them to suit your skills and those of your fellow players. If you have no chalk, look for a whitish rock with which you can scratch the

Diagram 2.6

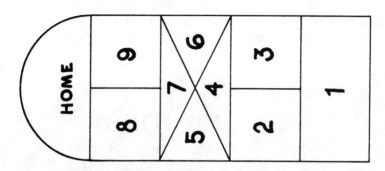

diagram onto the pavement. If you have no pavement, look for an area of hard-packed dirt and etch the diagram with a sharp stick.

HOPSCOTCH is a great solitaire pastime, but more often than not it is played by two, three, or four players, each of whom usually has his own hopscotch heel. If you

Diagram 2.7

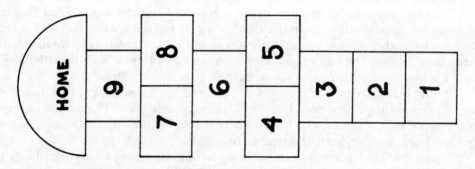

can't find a heel, any flat stone or piece of wood will suffice, as it did in olden times, before shoe heels became commonplace items.

Decide who will go first and establish an order of play. A player begins the game by standing at the bottom of the diagram and tossing his heel into the square marked "1." The player must hop all the way through the diagram, stop in the square containing the heel on the way back, bend over, pick up the heel, and exit. If a player misses the square on the toss or loses his balance or steps on a line or fails to retrieve the heel properly, his turn ends. Otherwise he continues by tossing his heel into the "2" square. When it becomes a player's turn again, he begins trying for the number he missed on his previous turn.

The object is to be the first player to make it through all the spaces on the diagram. In moving through the spaces, a player alternately lands on both feet and on one foot. So, in the first two diagrams above, you hop to space 1 on one foot, land in 2 and 3 with both feet, hop to 4 on one foot, land in 5 and 6 on both feet, hop to 7 on one foot, land in 8 and 9 on both feet, and hop to HOME on one foot. A player may not change his hopping foot during the game, but must stick with either the left or the right foot, whichever he prefers.

Optional rules add a special method of retrieving the heel from the last space on the diagram: It must be kicked to the base of the diagram while hopping on one foot. When standing within a space on one foot, a player is free to hop around, kicking the heel to adjust its position, so long as he does not touch a line, kick the heel out of the diagram, or lose his balance and fall. In retrieving the heel by this method, the player may kick it all the way out with one kick, or nudge it along as he hops. In either case, the heel must end up at the base of the diagram, and it must not land on any line or exit the diagram from the sides.

EGG JOUSTING

PLAYERS: *two*
LOCATION: *outdoors*
EQUIPMENT: *hard-boiled eggs*
SPECIAL SKILL: *none*

At spring feasting celebrations in Afghanistan and Russia, children delight in the sport of EGG JOUSTING, a tricky undertaking at best, which holds this single thought in the head of every spectator: "When will the egg break?"

To play, you need to hard-boil some eggs carefully so that their shells don't crack. Thrill seekers should play with raw eggs, wearing old clothes. Afghani and Russian children pay careful attention to dyeing their eggs, and the traditional color is red, perhaps for high visibility. You may use any bright color you like, and by all means, decorate your egg. The fancier your egg the more careful you'll likely be with it. And *careful* is the name of this game if you haven't guessed that already.

Before I describe how to play, you need a little egg terminology. The "head" of the egg means the pointed end. The "heel" is the rounded end. Thus, if you brought two players' eggs together, end to end, there would be three distinct combinations: head to head, head to heel, and heel to heel.

Determine which player goes first. That player must deliver a verbal challenge to the other player in the form of "With my heel I will break your heel" or "With my head I will break your head" or "With my heel I will break your head" or "With my head I will break your heel." It is up to the player and his knowledge of his own egg's strengths to determine which challenge to deliver.

The opponent evaluates this challenge. If it seems fair and he thinks he has a good chance of winning, he responds to the challenge with "Then, break it." He must now hold his egg cupped in his hand so that a portion of the challenged end of the egg shows through the circle made by thumb and forefinger. Now it is the original challenger's turn to evaluate the situation. If he feels he has a good chance, he strikes the portion of the opponent's egg that is showing. If he cracks it, the opponent must turn the egg upside down and show the other end, allowing the challenger another shot. If the challenged egg does not crack, the round ends, and the second player makes a new challenge to the first.

The player doing the challenging may feel the opponent is not showing enough of his egg, and is allowed to complain, "You're not showing much." A bit more of the egg must be revealed. The challenging player always has the option of turning the tables by responding, "I will show you more than that." At this point, the players' eggs are traded and the challenger becomes the challenged. He must keep true to his word and reveal more of the egg than his opponent did. Of course, it is to his advantage to reveal as much of the egg as the other player will allow, because although eggs have been traded, the original owner is still hoping his egg will survive the joust.

EGG JOUSTING is really a war of nerves and bravado between the players, as each hopes to deliver challenges he will win without being counterchallenged in the process.

When both ends of a player's egg have been cracked, the player may bring in a replacement egg or quit. Score is kept on the number of eggs "captured," though broken eggs are usually left behind. Survivors are eaten. If you win, please share the bounty with the loser.

KULIT K'RANG

PLAYERS: *any number*
LOCATION: *anywhere*
EQUIPMENT: *supply of small seashells or pebbles*
SPECIAL SKILL: *dexterity*

This game of dexterity and coordination has been played by children throughout Southeast Asia for many centuries. The variation described here comes from Indonesia. Any number can play; all you need is a bowl of small shells, beans, pebbles, or other suitable objects. Indonesian children play with small cockleshells.

There are two main ways of playing. In the first, players sit down in a circle, each with the same number of shells—fifteen or twenty is a good number. A bowl is placed in the center of the circle. In turn, each player places a shell on the back of his hand, tosses it into the air, and attempts to grab another shell from his lap and then catch the falling shell.

If the player succeeds in catching both shells in his hand, he keeps them in the pile in his lap. If not, one of the shells is contributed to the bowl in the center of the circle. When a player has no more shells, he drops out of the game. The last player remaining is the winner.

The second way to play goes like this: Start the game with extra shells in the bowl (about twenty or twenty-five). When a player succeeds on his turn, he may take one shell from the bowl. When he fails, he must contribute one of his own shells to the bowl. The winner is the player holding the greatest number of shells when none are left in the bowl.

BLOW FOOTBALL

PLAYERS: *two to six*
LOCATION: *table*
EQUIPMENT: *playing board, Ping-Pong ball, straws*
SPECIAL SKILL: *none*

This game, of unidentifiable origins, though definitely an American invention, is extremely popular with children under the age of twelve, and it will accommodate two teams of one, two, or three players per team. You must build your own playing board, but the endless hours of fun it will provide far outweigh the fifteen minutes it will take to build the board.

All you need is a flat piece of plywood or other lumber three to four feet long and two to two and a half feet wide, plus enough one-inch-high wood trim—the kind you see around the perimeter of a door or window—to make a border around the outside edges of the piece of plywood. Nail the trim to the edges of the plywood, leaving a six-inch gap at each end of the board as illustrated in Diagram 2.8. These gaps are the goals. You could also make a four-player board by leaving a six-inch gap in all four sides.

Diagram 2.8   BLOW FOOTBALL

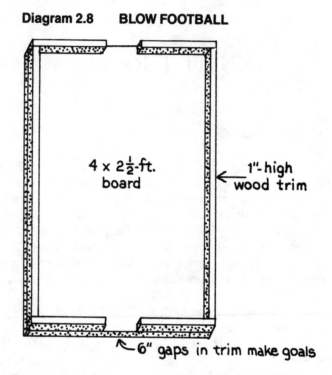

The ball used in BLOW FOOTBALL is an ordinary Ping-Pong ball, and the propellant is air: each player is armed with an ordinary drinking straw. The ball is placed in the center of the table, and on the word "GO!" players try to force the ball through the opponent's goal by blowing through their straws and aiming the streams of air at strategic points on the ball. No player may cross the midfield line or interfere with an opponent.

Points are scored when the ball passes through the goals, and play continues to an agreed-upon victory number or for a limited time period, whichever limitation players would rather use. If a player succeeds in blowing the ball over an edge of the playing field and out of bounds, the opposing team gets the equivalent of a free kick in soccer from the point where the ball left the field.

STORK FIGHTS

PLAYERS: *two*
LOCATION: *wherever ground or floor is soft*
EQUIPMENT: *scarf or long piece of cloth*
SPECIAL SKILL: *balancing*

This is an active competition for two players who don't mind a few small scrapes and bruises. Tie a single scarf or piece of cloth (never use rope) around the left ankles of two players. In unison, the players raise their joined left feet and at the word "GO!" they begin the struggle.

The loser is the player whose left foot touches the ground first. Other than that, it's anything goes. Sometimes players go off balance and fall to the ground, but the contest does not end until someone's left foot touches the ground. Of course, it doesn't take long to produce a winner when you're wrestling around on the ground.

INDIAN WRESTLING

PLAYERS: *two*
LOCATION: *wherever ground or floor is soft*
EQUIPMENT: *scarf or long piece of cloth*
SPECIAL SKILL: *balancing*

This game is similar to STORK FIGHTS in that you tie two players together at their right ankles with a scarf or cloth. Its origins lie in the lore of the American Indian, among whose braves and would-be braves it was a time-honored tradition. This native game of strength and dexterity is worth learning and passing on to future generations as part of our heritage.

The players must keep their tied feet on the ground and in the starting position at all times. At the signal "GO!" players use their hands, body weight, and free leg to maneuver the other player into a position where a part of his body other than his feet touches the ground.

If you can't tie the players' legs together or if you don't want to, another way to lose becomes moving your right foot from its starting position.

SHOVE WINTER OUT

PLAYERS: *eight or more*
LOCATION: *outdoors*
EQUIPMENT: *none*
SPECIAL SKILL: *shoving*

This game of physical endurance, of balance and coordination, originated with the Indians of Tierra del Fuego, a small group of islands at the southern tip of South

America, where winter governs sternly for much of the year. And as Indian children wait patiently for the bitter cold to pass, they amuse themselves with wishful thinking that they might be able to "shove winter out" early.

The game requires no equipment and should be played out of doors on a soft surface. Deep snow happens to be ideal. Don't play inside unless you have a large wrestling mat. SHOVE WINTER OUT will accommodate any number of players, though at least four or five are needed for each team. But, please, no one who can't stand a bruise or two.

First, divide the players into two groups: one for winter weather and one for summer. Members of each team should be easily identifiable. Indian children mark winter players' foreheads with a piece of charcoal.

Draw a circle of about twelve to fifteen feet in diameter. The players representing winter weather are positioned inside the circle to begin the game; summer-weather players remain outside. All players must fold their arms across their chests and keep them folded for the duration of the game. Any player unfolding his arms must drop out of the game.

The object for the summer-weather players is to shove the winter-weather players out of the circle, using only their backs and their shoulders. When a winter-weather player is forced outside the circle, he joins the summer team in trying to knock the others out.

At the end of the round, summer and winter players reverse roles and play again.

NECK-TARINES

PLAYERS: *any number*
LOCATION: *anywhere*
EQUIPMENT: *one or more nectarines (or any fruit)*
SPECIAL SKILL: *none*

Yes, it's an unusual spelling of the word "nectarines," but then, NECK-TARINES is an unusual game. It is also fun for any age group, and age and skill levels can be mixed. I can think of *no* group of players who shouldn't try this wonderful icebreaker.

You may play NECK-TARINES as a single team of any number of players, just to see if you can complete the task. Or you may divide into teams and compete against one another. It really makes no difference so far as the fun is concerned. Just make sure you stop when the laughter becomes painful.

Each team forms a line, and each player must clasp his two hands behind his back. Place a nectarine or an orange or a tangerine or even a lemon under the chin of the first player in each team's line. At the signal "GO!" the player with the fruit attempts to pass it to the next player in line, who must somehow grab it with his chin, neck, and upper chest. No other parts of the body are allowed to touch the fruit at any point during the game. If the fruit hits the floor or if a player cheats, the fruit is returned to the first player in the line, and passing it begins again.

If you are playing as one single team, the object is simply to pass the fruit down the line as quickly as possible. Time yourselves and keep trying to beat your record.

If you are playing competitively, the first team to successfully pass the fruit to its last player wins. Psychological warfare is a big part of the competitive version. Just as a member of the other team is about to successfully transfer the fruit makes a great time to tell a joke, particularly if you know one about fruit!

CHAPTER THREE
Target and Ball Games

Target and ball games are popular the world over for their combination of required skills. Not only must the player exhibit physical coordination, but he must combine this with mental strategy to overcome the physical skills of his opponents. These games are unlike those in Chapter One, because there is little or no player-to-player contact. The physical skills in the target and ball games are used to propel or catch inanimate objects, not to push, tackle, tag, or grab the other players.

The games in this chapter offer diverse challenges and differ widely in flavor, from the sedate steadiness of HORSESHOES to the frantic scrambling of STICKBALL, so children may always find the level of excitement and activity they desire. Several may be played indoors, but the majority were designed as compelling excuses for players to take in the sunshine and fresh air.

You'll find games for two, for four, for small teams, and for large groups. Some will be familiar, gathered from American streets and playgrounds; others come from foreign cultures. But all have at least one thing in common: aiming and propelling or maneuvering an object in some manner toward a target or group of targets.

DODGEBALL

PLAYERS: *ten or more*
LOCATION: *outdoors*
EQUIPMENT: *large rubber ball*
SPECIAL SKILLS: *throwing, dodging, catching*

DODGEBALL is an exhilarating, fast-paced, physical game of coordination and speed, and children have likely enjoyed some variation of it since the invention of the ball. It is a team sport for a large group of at least ten players (more if available), requiring a large rubber ball such as a volleyball or a soccer ball.

First, divide the group into two equal teams and mark out the boundaries. Draw two parallel lines about twenty-five feet apart, with a dotted line down the center. Each team occupies one half of the area. Sidelines may be drawn wherever you like, based on the number of players in the game. The more players the wider you should make the sidelines.

Members of each team must remain within their half of the playing field at all times during the game—this means no crossing over the dotted centerline and no stepping outside the boundaries, except to retrieve a wildly thrown ball.

Gather each team within its area, decide which team will go first, and give that team the ball. Now the teams begin alternately throwing the ball at each other. Players on the team being thrown at may try to dodge or catch the ball. A player who is hit by the ball is out of the game. But if a player catches the ball, then the thrower is out of the game. This creates great excitement and anticipation about each throw of the ball.

Thus, players are always tempted to position themselves directly in the path of the ball in hopes of catching it and putting the other player out of the game. But, to do this, a player must risk his own neck.

VARIATIONS

A standard variation for this game is to use more than one ball, which makes the action that much more frantic. But if you're looking for the most exciting action possible, try a variation called BOMBARDMENT.

BOMBARDMENT is played exactly the same as regular DODGEBALL, with one exception: when a player is called out of the game, he takes a place just *behind* the other team's back line. From then on, any ball the team misses may be caught by this player, who may then throw it back at the opponents. In this way, teams are forced to dodge balls coming from both directions: in front and behind!

SPUD

PLAYERS: *four or more*
LOCATION: *street or playground*
EQUIPMENT: *large bouncing ball*
SPECIAL SKILLS: *running, catching, throwing, dodging*

Who knows where the game of SPUD originated? Perhaps it was in Idaho? Maine? Anyway, I will never forget this game, which my sister and I and our friends would play for hours at a time during our preteen years. Much of the attraction is its easy-to-remember rules and small equipment list: one bouncing ball.

You'll need at least four players to make this game fun and lively, and certainly the more the merrier. One person holds the ball and the others gather around him. He then throws the ball high into the air directly over the group and simultaneously shouts the name of a player (the spud) who must try to catch the ball. Meanwhile, everyone runs frantically in another direction.

As soon as the spud has control of the ball, he shouts, "Spud!" and all must freeze in their tracks. The spud is then allowed to take four giant steps toward any player. He counts off the four steps by announcing the letters "S-P-U-D." The spud then tries to hit his intended victim with the ball, while the victim is not allowed to move except in trying to catch the ball. If the spud hits the victim, the victim is branded—well, not actually branded!—but he accumulates the letter *S*. If the ball misses the intended victim or if it is caught, the spud is given the letter *S*.

After each round, everyone gathers around the spud, who is the player that received a letter during the previous round of play, and the game begins again. A player remains in the game until he has collected all four letters, *S-P-U-D,* by being hit with the ball or missing on the throw four times. The last player remaining is the winner.

VARIATIONS

One of our favorite ways to play this game went under the name of THIS MEANS WAR!, in which each player assumed the name of a country. We would outline a large circle with chalk in the middle of the street or playground, sectioning it into a "pie," with the names of all the countries chalked inside the pieces of the circle. Our rule was that each player had to start a round standing in the country of his choice—one player to a country. This, of course, has nothing to do with the play of the game.

The only difference between this variation and standard SPUD is that the thrower is allowed to bounce the ball by smashing it into the concrete. Yes, this makes the ball more difficult to catch, but we liked it that way because our games lasted longer.

THE BRASS RING GAME

PLAYERS: *two or more*
LOCATION: *wherever you are able*
EQUIPMENT: *large brass ring, string, target with hooks*
SPECIAL SKILL: *aiming*

Although this target game rose to popularity during the reign of Queen Victoria, it is actively played to this day in pubs and school yards throughout England and many other parts of the world. It is also known as Ring the Bull and by several other names, and there are hundreds of variations on the rules. The game has its origin in another target game called Quoits. Presented below is a fairly standard version of the game, which you can make yourself quite easily.

Cut a triangle, square, diamond, circle, or other shape from a piece of wood. The

Diagram 3.1   THE BRASS RING GAME

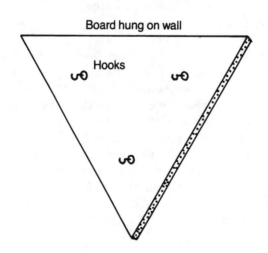

Diagram 3.2

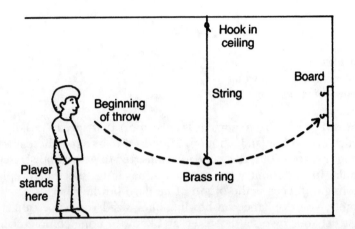

shape is not important, but the size should not exceed that of a trash-can lid. If you like, you may paint or paste a picture of a bull's head and horns on the board, as is done in England. Next, screw three hooks into the board in a triangular arrangement as shown in Diagram 3.1. In England, one hook goes on each horn and the third on the bull's nose.

Now you need a brass ring. In olden times, farmers used the actual rings from the noses of their bulls, but you can consider that unnecessary. Just get a solid brass ring about two inches in diameter and attach it to a long piece of string. See Diagram 3.2. Attach the board to the wall. Hold one end of the string on the ceiling about six feet away from the target, and have someone else stretch the string so that there is just enough room to hook the ring. Too much string will cause the ring to bounce off the wall. Too little will not allow the ring close enough to catch on a hook. Experiment with this distance until you get a good challenge.

The game will accommodate any number of players, but a small group of two or three is best. Decide who will go first and how many chances each player will have on each turn. Ten swings of the ring per turn is usually enough.

Players now take turns aiming and swinging the suspended ring at the target, with the object of hooking the ring on the bull's nose (or the lower target) as many times as possible. A player receives one point for each time he hooks the ring on the bull's nose. No points are awarded for ringing the bull's horns.

The game continues in this manner to a preset number of points, the first player to reach that total being the winner.

QUILLES

PLAYERS: *any number*
LOCATION: *wherever it may be set up*
EQUIPMENT: *nine pins, ball, rope*
SPECIAL SKILL: *aiming*

The game of QUILLES is an ancient French sport that spread rapidly throughout Europe, particularly to England, about five hundred years ago, where it was known as Kayles. During the late 1700s, the game was imported to America by Dutch settlers. It became popular in this country for a time, but has long since been replaced by the sport of bowling. QUILLES is the origin of modern bowling.

Fortunately, you don't need a bowling-alley-sized room for QUILLES. You will have to construct your own set, however, as I know of none commercially available. Still, this is fairly easy. You'll need ten by ten feet of playing space, so most often this game is played outdoors.

To make the game, first find something like a tree limb or barn rafter from which you can suspend a rope about ten feet up. If none is available, firmly plant a four-by-four wooden post in the ground with another across its top, in the shape of a T, as shown in Diagram 3.3.

Diagram 3.3   **QUILLES**

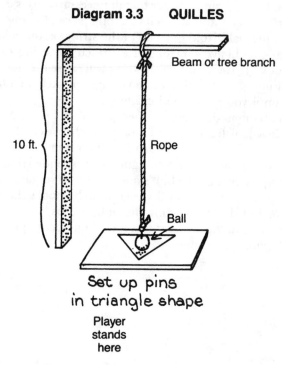

Beam or tree branch

10 ft.

Rope

Ball

Set up pins
in triangle shape

Player
stands
here

Tie the rope to the "T" or over the rafter or tree limb, and attach a round weight to the bottom of the rope so that it doesn't quite hit the ground when it swings back and forth. The weight should be the weight, size, and shape of a softball. (Hint: it's easy to screw a hook into an old softball, which gives you a place to attach the rope.)

Now, directly beneath the rope, place a three-foot-square board on which you will stand up an arrangement of nine bowling pins as shown in Diagram 3.4. You can use blocks of wood or empty plastic soda bottles partially weighted with wax or sand or anything else instead of bowling pins. The central pin should be shorter or heavier than the others to make it more difficult to knock down. This central pin is known as the "kingpin."

Diagram 3.4   QUILLES: PIN SETUP

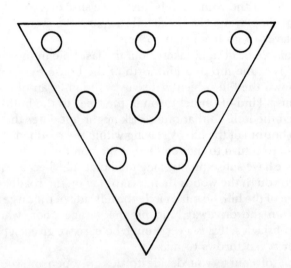

The game accommodates as many players as you have; if you're playing with more than five or six, use a scorecard to keep track of progress. Each player in turn grabs the ball and swings it toward the pins, hoping to knock down as many as possible. Another player or two should always be ready to catch the ball before it returns on the backswing. The ball is given only one chance to hit the pins.

Score one point for each of the eight outer pins knocked down, and a full nine points for the center pin, or kingpin. Determine in advance the number of rounds, or frames, you will play. The winner is the player at the end of those rounds who has the highest point score.

DISK GOLF

PLAYERS: *any number, two to four at a time*
LOCATION: *outdoors*
EQUIPMENT: *flying disks for all players*
SPECIAL SKILL: *throwing accuracy*

DISK GOLF, often referred to as Frisbee Golf, is one of my personal favorite outdoor sports games, because it offers the player so much freedom in creating his own course and guidelines of play. I have played on specially designed championship courses with regulation targets and hard-and-fast rules, and it's a lot of fun. But, to tell the truth, the course my friends and I designed in the woods around our house is even more fun.

DISK GOLF can be played by any number, but as in the sport of golf, a foursome is generally the maximum. More players just tend to get in one another's way. If you have more than four, split into groups as they do on the golf course. Each player will need his own flying disk. The object is to reach a goal from a starting point in the minimum number of throws.

The first thing you must do is design your course and decide how many holes, or targets, it will have. You may play with or without boundaries or special obstacles— that's entirely up to you and your friends. Just make sure everyone knows the ground rules before you begin playing. Give each hole a "par": the average number of throws it takes a good player to go from start to finish.

Here's an example of design, taken from the last hole in the course around our house. The "tee" is at the top of a hill north of the house by about three hundred yards. Winding down the hill, which is heavily wooded, is an old, unused roadbed. The roadbed forms a kind of tunnel through the trees to the bottom of the hill. We originally designed the hole so that one's disk might not enter the woods, but must travel from top to bottom of the hill by staying within the roadbed. A disk that flew off into the woods had to return to the roadbed at the point of its departure for another throw. However, we have subsequently amended that rule, because it is more difficult to throw the disk through the woods than it is to stay on the roadbed. When a player reaches the bottom of the hill, he must circle the left side of the large maple tree in the front yard, go down the driveway, and hit the garage door, which is the target. Because of all the obstacles, this is a very tough hole, so we give it a par five. Most new players take six or seven throws to make it.

Whatever type of course you decide to design, open or wooded, winding or straight, easy or difficult, make sure you define a starting line, or "tee," and an ending for each hole, as well as the ground rules. Regulation courses use something like a low-hung basketball net as the target for each hole. But there are lots of things that will do just as well: a fork in a tree, a garbage can, a sandbox, the patio, a large rock, the license plate on Dad's car . . .

LES BOULES

PLAYERS: *two to four*
LOCATION: *outdoors*
EQUIPMENT: *one ball per player*
SPECIAL SKILL: *throwing accuracy*

This very old French game is cousin to the game of Bowls, extremely popular in England for more than the past thousand years and dating back some three or four thousand years in Middle Eastern cultures. Bowls and the fancily manicured bowling greens are still taken *very* seriously in clubs throughout the world, with high-stakes tournaments regularly conducted on exquisitely cared-for grass playing fields. Dedicated players show a passion rivaled only by players of the Italian game of *Bocce*. In fact, on July 9, 1588, Sir Francis Drake insisted on finishing his game of Bowls before sailing out from Plymouth to engage the Spanish Armada.

From France and England, the two games reached the American colonies as early as 1720. To this day there are more than one hundred clubs in the American Lawn Bowling Association alone. Despite its allure, the game of Bowls requires a very expensive-to-maintain playing field and is refereed under a strict set of playing rules. Thus, it is somewhat restrictive to the rest of us, who would like to play in our backyards and parks.

Well, you can, thanks to LES BOULES. You can find commercially available sets under the Americanized name of Lawn Bowling. Lawn Bowling balls are softball-sized. In fact, you may use softballs if you wish, but each player will need a pair that are similarly colored. You also need what is known as the "jack," a smaller ball. A tennis ball will do nicely.

The game is usually played by two or four players, sometimes with players acting as partners. Select one player to go first and an order of play for everyone else. The first player takes the jack (the smaller ball), turns to face the other players, and throws it backward over his shoulder as far as he likes.

Each player in turn now throws or rolls his first ball, trying to get it as close as possible to the jack. Then each player in turn throws or rolls his second ball, again trying to get it or his other ball or those of his partner nearest to the jack. It is perfectly legal, and excellent strategy, to knock an opponent's ball farther from the jack or to knock yours or your partner's closer.

The player or team with the ball closest to the jack wins the round, scores one point toward an agreed-upon total, and gets to throw the jack and go first for the next round. The first player or team to reach the agreed-upon total wins.

Under optional rules, this game may be played within a restricted playing area, a rectangular lawn court of twenty by thirty feet, marked off with lime.

PIN

PLAYERS: *three to five*
LOCATION: *outdoors*
EQUIPMENT: *wooden pin, three to five balls*
SPECIAL SKILLS: *aiming, teamwork*

This cooperative variation on bowling is popular among the children of Guatemala, though this may not be its origin. It is a most interesting game for its heavy emphasis on cooperation with other players, designed for only one team of players at a time. There is no competitive version of PIN to my knowledge.

The game will accommodate from three to five players—more just makes it confusing. You will need a wooden pin, such as a bowling pin, or something to simulate it, like an empty plastic soda bottle weighted with wax. You will also need a ball for each player. The perfect ball would come from a *Bocce* or Lawn Bowling set, but you could use softballs or other large, round, heavy objects.

Set the pin a good distance from a starting line, say about twenty to thirty feet away. (You can experiment until you find a distance that is neither too easy nor impossible.) The object is to touch the pin with one of the balls *without* knocking the pin over. This is performed in the following manner.

The first player throws or rolls his ball as near the pin as possible. This becomes the lead ball, and it is the one that must touch the pin to win the game. The other players in turn roll their balls with the aim of knocking into the lead ball and advancing it closer to the pin. Once all players have thrown their balls, players move to the balls and throw again.

Play continues until the lead ball rests against the pin, which signifies success, or until the pin is knocked over, which signifies failure.

HORSESHOES

PLAYERS: *two to four*
LOCATION: *outdoors*
EQUIPMENT: *two stakes, four to eight horseshoes*
SPECIAL SKILLS: *throwing, aiming*

HORSESHOES is a competitive pastime that likely rose to popularity with farmers the world over because it makes use of objects found on nearly every farm: horseshoes. The game usually involves two players, or two teams of two players. These days, it's a bit more difficult to locate real horseshoes, but there are lots of commercially available sets if your town blacksmith has closed up shop in favor of a Toyota dealership.

The scoring posts used in horseshoes are wooden or iron rods, pounded firmly into the ground so that eight or ten inches shows. The two scoring posts should be placed twenty-five to forty feet away from each other. A throwing line is usually drawn two feet in front of each post. See Diagram 3.5.

Each player uses two similar horseshoes distinguished from his opponents' by markings or colors. Before you begin playing, decide how many points will win the

Diagram 3.5   HORSESHOES

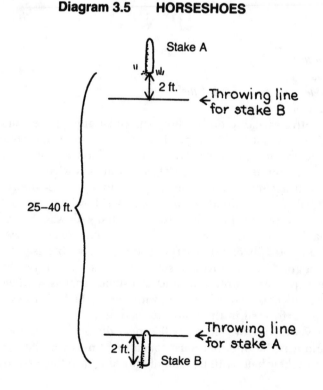

game, somewhere from ten to twenty-five. Then each player in turn throws his horseshoes, one at a time, toward the opposite scoring post. When all shoes have been thrown, the players walk to the post and score their throws.

Three points are awarded for each "ringer," which is a horseshoe that encircles the scoring post. Beyond that, one point is awarded for each horseshoe that is closer to the scoring post than an opponent's horseshoe. Diagram 3.6 shows the scoring after one round. The easiest way to score is to look at your shoe that is closest to the post. If your opponent's nearest shoe is farther away than yours, you score one point for that shoe. Then look at your other shoe. If your opponent's other shoe is closer to the post, he wins a point.

Diagram 3.6

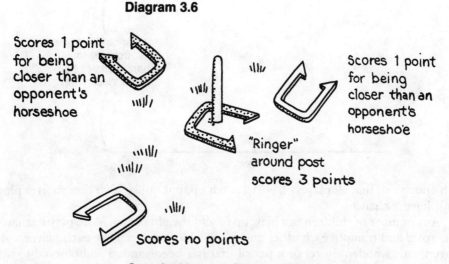

Scores 1 point for being closer than an opponent's horseshoe

Scores 1 point for being closer than an opponent's horseshoe

"Ringer" around post scores 3 points

Scores no points

Score for this round: Black-4, White -1

The maximum points a player can win on any turn is six, which is gotten by throwing two ringers. The first player or team to reach the agreed-upon total wins.

NUGLUTANG

PLAYERS: *three to ten*
LOCATION: *wherever you can hang the target*
EQUIPMENT: *target dowel, string, short dowels*
SPECIAL SKILL: *none*

The game of NUGLUTANG comes from Eskimo tribes living in the Arctic, where darkness comes for many boring months of the year. To while away some of that time, Eskimo children engage in a target game that was meant to be played indoors. Of course, NUGLUTANG is just as good outdoors, so long as your area of the world isn't dark at three o'clock in the afternoon!

Eskimos use a long, thin piece of caribou antler as the target. You will use a three-foot-long wooden dowel of three-quarters-inch diameter instead. Drill about a dozen quarter-inch holes along the dowel at random intervals. Suspend the target from the ceiling or from a tree limb by attaching a string to its center as shown in Diagram 3.7,

Diagram 3.7   NUGLUTANG

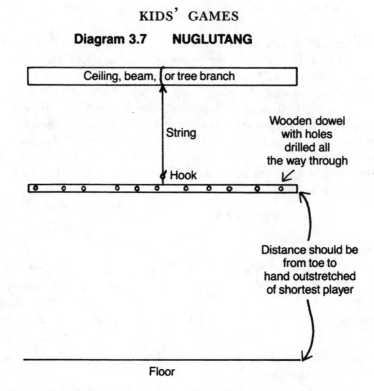

Ceiling, beam, or tree branch

String

Wooden dowel
with holes
drilled all
the way through

Hook

Distance should be
from toe to
hand outstretched
of shortest player

Floor

high enough so that all players have to reach up, but not so high that shorter players don't have a chance.

Any number of children can play, up to about eight or ten. More players than this just crowd and trample each other and no one has any fun. Give each player a short quarter-inch wooden dowel or a pencil that has been sanded and tapered to a dull point at each end. The object is to be the first player to stick his dowel through one of the holes in the target so that it does not fall right out.

Players drop out of the game as they succeed in landing their dowels within the target holes, and the game continues until the last player has done the same. As you might imagine, this game can take quite a while, because the suspended target doesn't stay still for anyone! It dips and bobs and swings around like crazy just above the heads of the laughing children.

The Eskimo children liven the game up by playing for interesting stakes. The first player to successfully insert his rod into the target must place some object of value on a table. This object becomes the property of the second player to succeed, who replaces the object with something of his own. In this way, the last player always wins something, but the winner, or first player, wins nothing!

STICKBALL

PLAYERS: *six to twelve*
LOCATION: *outdoors*
EQUIPMENT: *rubber ball, broom handle*
SPECIAL SKILLS: *hitting, running, throwing*

This game, obviously not the invention of some country boy, is the game of American baseball as it is played on city streets all over the country. Of course, every area adopts its own special rules, but the basic game is the same everywhere. STICKBALL, which can be played with any round bouncing ball and any lengthy slender stick, using whatever is handy for the playing field, proves out the old adage: necessity is the mother of invention.

First, divide the group into two equal teams of three to six players. Then agree on the four bases: sewer covers, tree stumps, lampposts, fire hydrants, old tires, or anything else you can find that makes a diamond shape from first to second to third to home.

Follow the rules of baseball for the rest of the game, with the following exceptions. The pitcher stands much closer than usual, about ten yards away, and pitches the ball underhand. Strikes and balls are not called; it is up to other players to nag a player who watches good pitches go by. If the ball is hit, no matter where (there is *no* foul territory), the batter runs as in baseball and can be forced or tagged out. Once on base, a runner is not allowed to move off the base until the ball is hit, and there is no stealing bases allowed. Most players agree that any ball caught, whether in the air or on the ground, makes an out.

You decide. It's your ball game!

STOOPBALL

PLAYERS: *four or more*
LOCATION: *against a set of stairs*
EQUIPMENT: *rubber ball*
SPECIAL SKILLS: *throwing, running, catching*

The inner-city game of STOOPBALL is a very popular pastime for teams of two to four frustrated ballplayers who usually find themselves without a ball field on which to play. STOOPBALL solves the problem while delivering every bit as much fun and strategy.

First, find a set of stairs outside and agree upon four targets across the street, such as walls, doorways, large signs, and so forth—just make sure they are unbreakable by the kind of ball you're using. Designate the easiest target as a "single," the next-most-difficult as a "double," then a "triple," and finally the "home run" target, which should be the most difficult to hit.

Divide into two even teams, and flip to see which team bats first. The other team should "take the field," which means they should stand between the stairs and the targets. In turn, players on the side that is up take the ball and throw it against the edge and sides of the lower steps, attempting to bounce it off one of the targets. The fielders try to catch or block each shot from reaching the targets.

Sides change from in the field to at bat when the fielding team has *caught* three hits, either grounders or fly balls. If the ball misses the targets and is not caught, there is no effect, and the next player on the team at bat steps up to the stoop for his turn. If the ball hits a target, both teams keep track of the imaginary runner. A man on second advances to third on a single, but is driven home on a double. Score is kept as in baseball.

Play continues until any agreed-upon number of innings.

STOOLBALL

PLAYERS: *five or more*
LOCATION: *outdoors*
EQUIPMENT: *any large bouncing ball and a stool*
SPECIAL SKILLS: *aiming, throwing, goal tending*

STOOLBALL came to the American colonies more than three hundred years ago from England, where it had enjoyed popularity among farmhands for who knows how long before that. The game is somewhat the country equivalent of STICKBALL and STOOPBALL, using equipment commonly found in farm country—the milking stool—as its only target.

Basically, you adjust all the rules to fit your particular group. If you have just a few players, you won't bother dividing into teams—you'll just vie for turns defending the stool. If you have a large group, divide into teams, and alternate players defending the stool among the teams. Give each team three to five "outs" before they must take to the field.

The game is simple. Draw or imagine a circle about ten feet in diameter and place the stool in the center. One player sits on the stool and the others gather around the edge of the circle, passing the rubber ball (a volleyball is good) from one player to the next. These players should try to confuse and disorient the player on the stool by moving the ball rapidly around the circle.

At will, any player may take a shot at the stool by throwing or rolling the ball toward it. The player sitting on the stool tries to prevent the ball from hitting any part of it by any means available without getting off the stool. If a player succeeds in hitting the stool, he takes over the duty of defending it. In team play, hitting the stool counts as one "out."

There is no score to keep in this game, so younger players will enjoy playing it until they drop.

PALM BALL

PLAYERS: *two to four*
LOCATION: *outdoors*
EQUIPMENT: *rope, tennis or rubber ball*
SPECIAL SKILLS: *aiming, hitting*

This ancient ancestor to tennis and handball was being played by Roman youngsters more than two thousand years ago as the Roman armies reached Spain, through which country it came to America via early explorers and became a part of Aztec culture. A Spaniard by the name of Francisco Cervantes de Salazar, a teacher, came to Mexico and codified many ball games, among them PALM BALL.

The game is designed, like tennis, for either two or four players, playing as singles or doubles against the other team. Draw a rectangular court or agree on existing boundaries, and tie a length of rope across the center of the area as in tennis. Each team positions itself within one half of the court and is not allowed to cross the rope boundary.

The ball is served with the hand by one team member, passing to the other the next time it is that team's serve. If the ball hits the rope on the serve, the ball is served again. If the ball goes out of bounds, the opposing team wins fifteen points. Otherwise, one of the players must hit it back with his hand before it bounces a second time. If the ball is returned under the net or out of bounds, the server wins fifteen points.

The ball may also be caught in the palm of the throwing hand and thrown back, but it will cost the player fifteen points if he attempts to catch the ball and drops it on his side of the court or out of bounds.

A game is played to forty-five points, and usually a match is set at six games.

CHAPTER FOUR
Music/Singing/Clapping Games

Children from all over the world love to sing, and for this reason traditional children's songs have always been incorporated into simple dancing, skipping, or running games. Children also love clapping and performing stunts to set rhythms.

The games below use musical rhythms accompanied by singing, clapping, ball-bouncing, and rope-skipping exercises. They encourage the coordination of vocal and manual dexterity, sometimes cooperatively and sometimes competitively among the players.

Learning and remembering the rules to these games is easy, even for young children. But many of the games use verses that many parents find difficult to remember from their childhoods. To help keep these games alive and well in the backyards and playgrounds of America, I've reproduced a few exemplary verses with the game rules. Pass these verses on to the next generation.

RING A RING OF ROSES

PLAYERS: *three or more*
LOCATION: *any soft surface*
EQUIPMENT: *none*
SPECIAL SKILL: *singing*

Young children will play this game for hours at a time, because there are no real losers and it's very easy to understand. Also, children love to sing the meaningless verse. Usually the game is sponsored by an adult or older player.

The children join hands forming a circle, then begin dancing in one direction while singing the following verse:

> Ring a ring of roses,
> A pocket full of posies,
> Ashes, ashes,
> We all fall down!

Upon the word "down," all players drop down to a sitting position while continuing to hold hands. That's all there is to it, except for several other verses:

> The king he sent his daughter
> To fetch a pail of water,

Ashes, ashes,
We all fall down!

The wedding bells are ringing.
The boys and girls are singing.
Ashes, ashes,
We all fall down!

The bird is in the steeple.
He's singing to the people.
Ashes, ashes,
We all fall down!

Some children like to play this game with the following variation: the first time through the song, they fall down at the end of the first verse only. The second time through, they fall down at the end of the second verse only, and so forth, falling down at the end of the next verse each time they sing through the song. The point is for players to remember when to fall down and when to keep dancing.

LONDON BRIDGE

PLAYERS: *eight or more*
LOCATION: *anywhere, usually outdoors*
EQUIPMENT: *none*
SPECIAL SKILLS: *singing, running*

Almost everyone can remember the first verse to the amusing children's song "London Bridge," which goes like this:

London Bridge is falling down,
Falling down, falling down.
London Bridge is falling down,
My fair lady.

But can you recite the rest? Or do you know how to play the game that has always been associated with the song? That's all right. Most people don't know or have forgotten how to play this game, despite its amazing popularity with young children. LONDON BRIDGE is a game of many things: of singing, of skipping and running, and of tug-of-war. It is best played with a large group of children, with eight as a minimum.

Two players are chosen to be the bridge keepers, and they clasp their hands together above their heads to form an arch through which all the other children will run or skip. The bridge keepers should stand far enough apart so that pairs of players, side by side, can fit between them under the arch. The remaining players should line up at one end of the bridge (which is actually a tunnel) in pairs. If you have an odd number of players, the first player to return to the end of the line will pair up with the lone player.

The bridge keepers and the other players alternate singing the verses to the song reprinted below as the pairs of children run or skip through the bridge then race to return to the end of the line and go through again. Sometime during the last verse ("Take the keys and lock them up"), the bridge keepers lower their arms and capture the pair of players currently trying to pass beneath the bridge. Players should not hesitate when they feel the bridge is about to lower but must try to scamper through.

When a pair of players is caught by the bridge keepers, one player stands behind one bridge keeper and the other player behind the other bridge keeper. The song is sung again and again until all players have been caught in this manner and divided into two equal teams. At this point, a rope is used to play tug-of-war between the two teams, the first team to drag the other over a centerline being the winner. If you don't have a rope, players grab the waist or belt of the player in front of them to form a human chain, with the first player of each team firmly grasping the hands of the other.

Here is the song "London Bridge":

> London Bridge is falling down,
> Falling down, falling down.
> London Bridge is falling down,
> My fair lady.
>
> How shall we build it up again,
> Up again, up again?
> How shall we build it up again,
> My fair lady?
>
> We will build with wood and clay,
> Wood and clay, wood and clay.
> We will build with wood and clay,
> My fair lady.
>
> But wood and clay will wash away,
> Wash away, wash away.
> Wood and clay will wash away,
> My fair lady.
>
> We will build with iron and steel,
> Iron and steel, iron and steel.
> We will build with iron and steel,
> My fair lady.
>
> But iron and steel will bend and break,
> Bend and break, bend and break.
> Iron and steel will bend and break,
> My fair lady.
>
> We will build with silver and gold,
> Silver and gold, silver and gold.
> We will build with silver and gold,
> My fair lady.
>
> But silver and gold will be stolen away,
> Stolen away, stolen away.
> Silver and gold will be stolen away,
> My fair lady.
>
> We'll put a man to watch all night,
> Watch all night, watch all night.
> We'll put a man to watch all night,
> My fair lady.
>
> Suppose the man should fall asleep,
> Fall asleep, fall asleep.
> Suppose the man should fall asleep,
> My fair lady.

Take the keys and lock him up,
Lock him up, lock him up.
Take the keys and lock him up,
My fair lady.

THREE BLIND MICE

PLAYERS: *six or more*
LOCATION: *large, open room*
EQUIPMENT: *none*
SPECIAL SKILL: *none*

This game might well be classified with tag and other chase games, as that is its ultimate object. But children seem to love it because singing the song is such a fun part of the game. The song may be silly, but the game is lots of fun for your youngest players. And it requires no equipment or special skills. You'll need at least six players and a medium-size playroom. Or play outdoors using distinct square boundaries about the size of a room.

Select one child to play the part of the farmer's wife. Everyone else should join hands and form a large circle around the farmer's wife. To begin the game, everyone begins dancing in one direction, singing the song:

Three blind mice, three blind mice.
See how they run. See how they run.
They all run after the farmer's wife,
Who cut off their tails with a carving knife.
Did you ever see such a sight in your life
As three blind mice?!

On the last word of the song, the players let go of each other and run in all directions. The farmer's wife runs after them, trying to tag one. Any player who reaches a wall or boundary without being tagged is safe. The first player tagged becomes the farmer's wife for the next game. But if the farmer's wife doesn't catch anyone, she must try again.

THE FARMER'S IN THE DEN

PLAYERS: *eight or more*
LOCATION: *anywhere*
EQUIPMENT: *none*
SPECIAL SKILL: *none*

This is another simple children's singing game with origins somewhere in the Midwest a hundred years ago or so. You need a group of eight or more players, but no equipment or special skills are required. Except, of course, the ability to remember the song! That's where this book comes in handy.

Select one child to play the part of the farmer. The other players join hands forming a circle around the farmer, and begin dancing in one direction while singing the following song:

> The farmer's in the den.
> The farmer's in the den.
> Heigh-ho-a-dairy-o,
> The farmer's in the den.

> The farmer needs a wife.
> The farmer needs a wife.
> Heigh-ho-a-dairy-o,
> The farmer needs a wife.

During the last verse, above, the farmer selects another player and points to him. Without breaking the rhythm of the singing or the motion of the dancing, the other player joins the farmer in the center of the circle.

> The wife needs a child.
> The wife needs a child.
> Heigh-ho-a-dairy-o,
> The wife needs a child.

During the above verse, the player chosen as the wife selects another player from the circle to be the child, who, at the end of the verse, lets go of the hands and joins the farmer and the wife in the circle.

> The child needs a nurse.
> The child needs a nurse.
> Heigh-ho-a-dairy-o,
> The child needs a nurse.

During the above verse, the child selects a nurse.

> The nurse needs a dog.
> The nurse needs a dog.
> Heigh-ho-a-dairy-o,
> The nurse needs a dog.

During the above verse, the nurse selects a dog.

> We all pat the dog,
> We all pat the dog,
> Heigh-ho-a-dairy-o,
> We all pat the dog.

During the above verse, the farmer, the wife, the child, and the nurse all pat the dog on the head. The dog is then the farmer for the next round and the game begins again.

PAT-A-CAKE

PLAYERS: *two*

LOCATION: *anywhere*

EQUIPMENT: *none*

SPECIAL SKILLS: *rhythmic clapping, singing*

This very simple children's game is a relative of clapping chants from Eastern Europe and throughout Asia, nonequipment games thousands of years old that still delight the young with their cooperative tasks. This is not a game in which you win unless both players win, or lose unless both players lose.

The game is played by two players seated facing one another up close, often a parent and young child. The rhyme sung by both players as they clap their hands in rhythm goes like this:

> **P**at a cake, **p**at a cake,
> **B**aker's **m**an.
> **B**ake me a **c**ake
> As **f**ast as you **c**an.
> **R**oll it and **p**at it
> And **m**ark it with a "**B**"
> And **p**ut it in the **o**ven
> For **b**aby and **m**e.

The boldface letters in the song indicate the places where each player claps his own two hands together. Between each of these you will clap either one or both of your hands palms outward against those of your partner, synchronized precisely if you can manage it.

There are four claps to the patterns you may devise on your own to use with the song.

1. Clapping your own two hands together.
2. Clapping your two hands against those of your partner.
3. Clapping your right hand to that of your partner.
4. Clapping your left hand to that of your partner.

Begin with a one-two-one-two-one-two . . . rhythm to establish singing and clapping at the same time. Then, as you become more coordinated, add the third and fourth claps to your rhythms. See how intricate you can get and still finish the song without any mistakes.

Try this game once before you condemn it as a baby's pastime!

MUSICAL CHAIRS

PLAYERS: *five or more*
LOCATION: *indoors*
EQUIPMENT: *one fewer chairs than you have players, a source of music*
SPECIAL SKILL: *alertness*

The game of MUSICAL CHAIRS has long been a favorite with American children. I have no reference to its being played in other countries, but I'm sure it is. You need a piano, radio, or some other source of music that can easily be started and stopped by the host of the party.

Children adore this game, probably because there are no skills involved, and the chances for success on each round seem good. Line the chairs up back to back forming two large rows or in a circle facing outward. The children parade around the perimeter of the chairs while the music plays. But as soon as the music stops—and it should stop abruptly and at intervals of random length—the children scamper to be seated in the nearest chair.

The one child left without a seat is out of the game. Also, one chair is removed, leaving one fewer than the number of players remaining in the game. The music starts again, the children begin parading around the chairs, and when the music stops they try to get a seat. Again, the child without a seat is out of the game and another chair is removed before the music recommences.

The game continues in this manner until the only chair left is sat in by one of the only two players left. The winner of that round wins the game.

To accommodate young children who don't enjoy being called "out" of the game when they lose, try this variation: prepare treats for all players, such as hot chocolate, but hand it out to each player as he leaves the game.

BOUNCING-BALL RHYMES

PLAYERS: *one or more*
LOCATION: *any hard surface*
EQUIPMENT: *bouncing ball*
SPECIAL SKILLS: *bouncing, catching, singing*

Most children are fortunate enough to have the best and most basic of playthings: a bouncing ball. Yet there are not always enough players for a ball game, and sometimes no one feels like competing. Then again, sometimes a player finds himself all alone with his bouncing ball. What kind of game could he play?

Bouncing-ball games, of course! Children are endless sources of simple rhymes, and for ages the rhythms of their silly verses have been used to accompany the bouncing of a ball off the ground. I'm sure you have plenty of rhymes you could put to work. But I'll give you a few to get things started.

Bouncie, Bouncie, Ballie
Bouncie, **b**ouncie, **b**allie.

My **s**ister's **n**ame is **P**aulie.
I **g**ave her a slap;
She **p**aid me back.
Bouncie, **b**ouncie, **b**allie.

In the song above, bounce your ball off the ground on the highlighted letters. There are, of course, other ways you can bounce the ball to this and the following rhymes. Feel free to make up your own bouncing rhythms.

My Mother Was Born in England
My **m**other was born in England.
My **f**ather was born in France.
But **I** was born in **d**iapers,
Because I had no **p**ants.

The object in the above rhyme is to set up a bouncing rhythm so that you can pass your leg over the bouncing ball on the highlighted letters.

One, Two, Three
One, **t**wo, **three**.
My **m**other **c**aught a **flea**.
She **s**alted it and **p**eppered it
And **g**ave it to **me** for **tea**!

In the above rhyme, set up a bouncing rhythm so that the ball hits the ground on the highlighted letters. On the last highlighted letter in the first, second, and last lines of the verse, pass your leg over the ball as it bounces off the ground. You bounce the ball only twice on the third line, and you do not pass your leg over the ball there.

Number One
Number one, touch your tongue.
Number two, touch your shoe.
Number three, touch your knee.
Number four, touch the floor.
Number five, act alive.
Number six, pick up sticks.
Number seven, go to heaven.
Number eight, shut the gate.
Number nine, touch your spine.
Number ten, do it again.

You can set up your own bouncing rhythm to the rhyme above. It's a tricky one, though, because you must act out each sentence as you bounce the ball. Use your nonthrowing hand to touch your tongue, shoe, knee, etc. Make up your own actions to simulate acting alive and going to heaven.

JUMP-ROPE

PLAYERS: *five or more*
LOCATION: *outdoors*
EQUIPMENT: *rope*
SPECIAL SKILLS: *jumping, timing*

Doing tricks while jumping a rope is incredibly popular with children, not to mention athletes who picked up on the serious exercise this seemingly childish game can bring. There are so many thousands of JUMP-ROPE games and tricks that all the pages in this book couldn't cover them. So I will describe several group JUMP-ROPE games that typify the fun and allure of this activity. You can find books in the library listing hundreds of other JUMP-ROPE games.

ALL IN TOGETHER

This popular variation provides simultaneous play for all jumpers, and is one of the best of its kind. You will need two rope turners; up to three or four jumpers may participate. Position the jumpers in a line next to the rope and have the turners begin to turn the rope. Let the rope turn a couple of times before the chanting begins:

> All in together, kids.
> How do you like the weather, kids?
> January, February, March, April,
> May, June, July, August, September,
> October, November, December.

The trick to this game is that each jumper must jump out of the rope when he hears the month of his birthday called. If everyone makes it outside without hitting the rope and stopping the game, keep the rope turning and begin the chant again. This time, the children jump back into the turning rope when they hear the months of their birthdays called.

DOWN THE MISSISSIPPI

This is a good game for a crowd of players, because everyone gets an equal chance to perform. The chant for this variation is only one line long:

"**D**own the Mississippi, where the **b**oats go **p**ush!"

The two rope turners turn the rope at a medium pace, hitting the ground on the four highlighted letters of the chant. The rest of the children line up, ready to leap into the rope and begin jumping. The first player in line is physically pushed into the rope by the player behind him on hearing the word "**p**ush" of the chant. This second player then jumps in, and the two players jump together until the word "**p**ush" is chanted again, at which time the first jumper is pushed out of the rope by the second, and the second jumper is joined by the next player in line.

This continues as long as desired, with players returning to the end of the line after their turns.

NAME CALLING

This is one of the most popular group JUMP-ROPE games, because each new jumper is allowed to call the name of the next jumper, who scrambles to jump in. Select one player to go first and have the rope turners begin turning the rope. The first player jumps in, jumps the rope twice, calls the name of any other player, waits for the new player to join him, jumps with the new player twice, then jumps out of the rope and rejoins the other players waiting for their turns.

With a large group, you can play with the rule that mistakes force a player out of the game. A mistake would be missing a jump, not responding fast enough when your name is called, or failing to exit the rope at the proper time. The first two players who get put out of the game should trade places with the rope turners to give them a chance to jump.

QUARTER TURNS

This trick is slightly more difficult than the previous ones. Two players begin turning the rope as the others form a line. One by one, players run in, jump once, make a quarter turn to the right, jump again, make another quarter turn, and so on until they are facing the same direction as when they entered. So each player makes four jumps, turning 90 degrees on each jump and jumping out of the rope on the last one.

MOTHER, MOTHER

This game is perfect for five players. Fewer won't do, though you may accommodate more than five by trading places with the rope turners every so often. The turners begin turning the rope, and the other players form a line ready to jump in one at a time. Here is the rhyme:

> **M**other, **m**other, **I** am **s**ick.
> **C**all for the **d**octor, **q**uick, **q**uick, **q**uick!
> **I**n came the **d**octor; **i**n came the **n**urse;
> **I**n came a **l**ady with an **a**lligator **p**urse.
> **O**ut went the **d**octor; **o**ut went the **n**urse;
> **O**ut went the **l**ady with the **a**lligator **p**urse.

The verse begins with one player jumping the rope on the highlighted letters above. He jumps alone for the first two lines. Then, on the first word of the third line, he is joined by a second player, who jumps along with him. In the middle of the third line, the two jumping players are joined by another, the nurse. And with the beginning of the fourth line, a fourth player runs in. These same players begin jumping out of the rope with the fifth and sixth lines, until no jumpers are left within the rope at the end of the verse.

STUNT JUMPS

There are thousands of tricks to perform while jumping rope, and they are often combined into a predefined sequence that a player must perform while reciting verse, as in the following variation:

> **O**ne, **t**wo, **t**ouch my shoe.
> **T**hree, **f**our, **t**ouch the floor.
> **F**ive, **s**ix, **c**riss-crossed sticks.
> **S**even, **e**ight, **d**ouble rate.
> **N**ine, **t**en, jump **o**ut again.

While reciting the above verse, the player must make his jumps on the highlighted letters. He must also perform a small trick in each line of the verse. At the end of the first, he touches his shoe. At the end of the second, he touches the ground. At the end of the third line, he crosses his legs on the jump. At the end of the fourth, the turners double the speed of the rope. Thus, the player jumps six times on the last line of the verse before jumping out of the rope and making room for the next player.

WHO, ME?

PLAYERS: *five or more*
LOCATION: *anywhere*
EQUIPMENT: *none*
SPECIAL SKILLS: *memory, reaction timing*

This game qualifies as both a memory response game and as a rhythmic music game, and young children love to play it over and over again. It requires no equipment or movement, with all action being spoken, and can be played anywhere, except the library or study hall! You'll need a group of at least five players, and the more the merrier in this game, up to about a dozen.

First, select one player to act as the leader. It is the leader's duty to keep the game going at an increasingly faster pace and to try to eliminate players one at a time by surprising and/or confusing them into giving a wrong answer or not answering at all. The game is occasionally accompanied by a clapping rhythm set up by the leader and followed by all other players. It is more difficult to keep your mind on the game when you are clapping your hands to a quickening rhythm, so try the game both ways.

Next, the leader assigns either numbers or letters or names or whatever is agreed upon to each of the other players. The players should take a moment to memorize their own numbers or letters or whatever as well as those of everyone else in the game.

The leader now begins the round, which goes something like this:

Leader:	Number 6.
Number 6:	Who, me?
Leader:	Yes, you.
Number 6:	Couldn't be.
Leader:	Then, who?
Number 6:	Number 3.

> Number 3: Who, me?
> Leader: Yes, you.
> Number 3: Couldn't be.
> Leader: Then, who?
> Number 3: Number 2.
> Number 2: Who, me?
> Leader: Yes, you . . .

And so the game continues, with the pace of the questions and answers becoming gradually faster until players begin making mistakes. If a player gives the wrong response or if he doesn't respond to his own number, he is disqualified from the round.

Play continues until there is only one player left to answer the leader's question. This player is the winner.

There are hundreds of these six-line response games and it's very easy to make up your own. Rhyming responses are best.

SECTION II:

Nonaction Games

CHAPTER FIVE
Word Games

Word games are among the most portable of all games. They travel anywhere, most of them requiring no equipment or action. Some, of course, require paper and pencil, but nothing else.

The best thing about word games, of course, is that they deal with words. The games help us learn more about our language and how it is put together. They improve our vocabulary, memory, and associative powers while providing lots of fun and laughter.

Word games are great for families, too, with older players helping the younger, less skillful players along. None of the games are very complicated, although a few such as CHARADES and CONVERSATION require somewhat sophisticated acting abilities. In any case, the games can all be tailored to the skill level and age range of the players.

These games aren't just fun, either. They can save your life. Literally. If you have young children, you understand what I mean. Don't take your next long-distance family car ride without at least one word game. It keeps everyone from getting on the driver's nerves and makes the miles seem to go by faster.

NO, NO!

PLAYERS: *any number*
LOCATION: *anywhere*
EQUIPMENT: *none*
SPECIAL SKILL: *rhyming*

I am a big fan of rhyming games, and NO, NO! is one of the best as well as one of the simplest. The game works as well with two players as it does with ten, and you won't need any equipment, special play area, or predetermined order of play. Just jump in whenever you can think of a new rhyming word.

The game begins with a definition as one player states a word, then gives a definition for a rhyming word, rather than the word itself. For example, I might start a game by saying, "Bear: this is something that grows on your body." Another player might continue, "No, No! You mean hair, which is a female horse." A third player might now contribute, "No, No! You mean mare, which is what doctors give their patients." I might jump back in now and say, "No, No! You mean care, which you do when you are very interested in something."

The object is to keep the chain of rhyming, misdefined words growing, and the last player able to add a rhyme to the chain wins the round.

If you like, you may play a more structured game in which players must sit in a circle and add to the chain in turn. A player who hesitates too long or who cannot think of a new rhyme at all is out of the game. The last player remaining, in this case, would be the winner.

TABOO

PLAYERS: *any number*
LOCATION: *anywhere*
EQUIPMENT: *none*
SPECIAL SKILLS: *spelling, vocabulary*

No one quite agrees on what kind of game TABOO is, but I call it a word game. TABOO calls for no equipment and accommodates any number of players of any age and skill range, so long as no one gets picked on unfairly. You have to be a good sport to be a good TABOO player.

First, select one player to be the first leader, and establish an order of play. (It would help to arrange all players in a circle, clockwise according to this order, but it isn't necessary.) The leader announces which letter of the alphabet will be taboo (forbidden) during this round. The other players memorize this letter.

Now the leader begins asking a question of each player in turn around the circle. The nature of the question is entirely up to the leader. The player must give a reasonable answer to the question *without using the taboo letter*. This means the letter may not be contained in any word used in answering the question. Nonsensical answers may be disqualified by a consensus of the players.

Here's an example of a fictitious round with four players in which the chosen taboo letter is *a*.

Leader (to the first player):   What would you do if I gave you a million dollars?
Player 1:   I would buy ten houses.
Leader (to the second player):   Why don't you like French food?
Player 2:   It gives me indigestion.
Leader (to the third player):   What planet are we living on?
Player 3 (after a short pause):   The third one from the sun.
Leader (to the fourth player):   What are your two favorite animals and why?
Player 4:   I like tigers, but monkeys give me even more excitement. Both look very lithe to me.

The other players think about this answer for a moment, but no one complains, so the round continues.

Leader (to the first player):   What kind of people work on a theater stage?
Player 1:   . . .

Player 1 hesitates too long trying to avoid the words "actor" and "actress," so he is disqualified from the round. Now there are only three players.

Leader (to the next player):   Where would you pitch a tent in the woods for the safest night's sleep?
Player 2:   Under the biggest pine tree I could find, because no wind would hit the tent.

At this point, the player is disqualified because he used the word "because," which contains an *a*.

Players are not allowed to hesitate in giving their answers, nor are they allowed to get away with a simple "yes" or "no." The group always decides democratically on the acceptability of another player's answer. Also, a player is not allowed to give an answer that is obviously out of character. It must be a reasonable response. To preserve the integrity of the game, the leader should ask easier questions of the younger, less skillful players, and more difficult questions of the older ones.

Each round of TABOO lasts until a single player remains and he is able to answer one last question from the leader. If he answers the last question without being disqualified, he is the winner and becomes the leader for the next round. Otherwise, players select a new leader in a manner of their own choosing.

TEAPOT

PLAYERS: *any number*
LOCATION: *anywhere*
EQUIPMENT: *none*
SPECIAL SKILL: *none*

This game appeals strongly to children, because it is designed to make them laugh. Also, any number can play and no special equipment is necessary. All you need is one player willing to be "It." TEAPOT is much like ADVERBS, except it is easier for young children to play.

First, send It out of the room and have the group decide upon a verb to be used as the basis for the game. Now call It back into the room and invite him to guess the verb everyone else has in mind. To do this, It receives clues by asking questions of the other players, substituting the word "teapot" for the verbs in the questions.

For example, let's say I am It and the group has decided on the verb "drive." Here's how some of the round might go:

I: Chris, where do you *teapot*?
Chris: All over town.
I: John, do you *teapot*?
John: No, I'm too young.
I: Tom, are you a good *teapotter*?
Tom: Very good. And that's no accident!
I: Chris, what would you do if I *teapotted* you now?
Chris: Sit back, relax, and take a nap.

The round would likely continue for quite some time before I guessed the verb.

However, that's not all there is to it: players must listen and respond to the questions without laughter. So, the funnier you can make the word *teapot* sound, the more successful you'll be. Any player who laughs is out of the game. In this manner, TEAPOT continues until the guesser has eliminated all other players by making them laugh or until he correctly identifies the verb.

JOTTO

PLAYERS: *two*
LOCATION: *anywhere*
EQUIPMENT: *pencil and paper*
SPECIAL SKILLS: *word building, logical deduction*

JOTTO is a word game of deductive logic hundreds of years old. It is a pencil-and-paper game for two players of any age and skill level. It is also the basis for the popular game of decoding colored pegs called Mastermind.

To begin a round, one player writes down a three-, four-, or five-letter word on the top of a piece of paper, then folds the paper so that the word cannot be seen. The player announces how many letters he is using in his hidden word, and a solving grid is set up. The example in Diagram 5.1 is for a three-letter word. The actual word itself has been written on the bottom of the sheet of paper, then the sheet was folded so it cannot be seen by the solver.

The other player now takes a guess at the word and writes his guess down in the first row under the column for guesses. The opponent compares the guess to his hidden word and gives clues to it in the responses column. The opponent puts down one *O* in the responses column for every correct letter that is also in the correct position in the word. The opponent also puts down one *X* for every correct letter that is *not* in the proper position in the word. If no letters are correct, no response is made.

The guesser examines the clues in the responses column, then formulates another guess at the word and writes it in the guesses column on the next row. Again the other player responds with how many letters are correct and how many in the correct position.

Keep track of the number of guesses. Then, when the word is guessed, switch places with the other player. The player taking the least number of guesses is the winner.

The following annotated example should help you understand how the game is played:

GUESSES	RESPONSES	
1. BARE	0	[one correct letter in correct place]
2. HARE	00	[two correct letters in correct places]
3. HERE	00	[two correct letters in correct places]
4. HERO	00	[two correct letters in correct places]
5. HURT	0000	[complete word guessed correctly]

Here's the logic behind the solving. With the first guess, we know that only one of our letters is correct, but it is in the correct position, too. We changed just one letter for the next guess, and the response was two correct letters in the correct place. Therefore, the word must begin with the letter *h,* and either the *a, r,* or *e,* is in the correct position.

We changed just one letter for the third guess and got the same response. This means the second letter of the word *cannot* be an *a* or an *e.* It also means that the letters *a* and *e* do not belong anywhere in the word; otherwise we'd have gotten an *X.* Because

Diagram 5.1   JOTTO

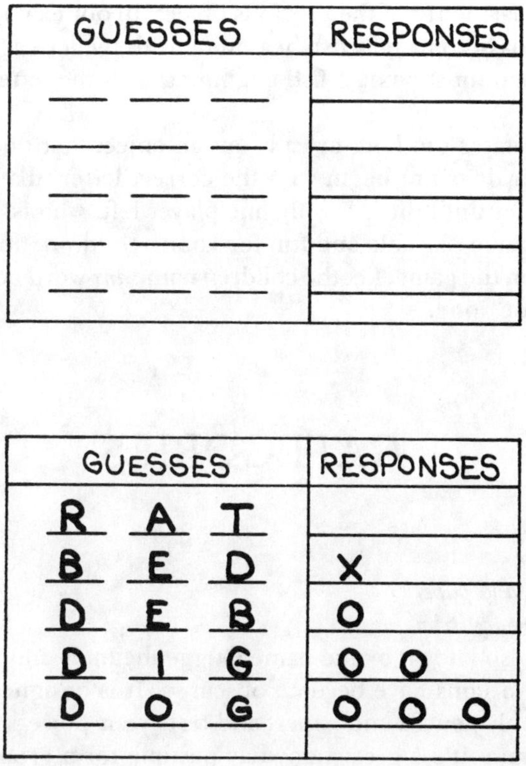

GUESSES	RESPONSES
__ __ __	
__ __ __	
__ __ __	
__ __ __	
__ __ __	

GUESSES	RESPONSES
R A T	
B E D	X
D E B	O
D I G	O O
D O G	O O O

we have eliminated the letters *a* and *e,* we can tell from the first and second guesses that the correct letters so far must be *h__r__*.

With the fourth guess we try to determine if *o* is part of the word. According to the response, it is not. The only vowels left are *i* and *u.* Since we can't think of any words ending with *U,* we figure that letter must go in the second position, giving us HUR__. We take a guess that the word is HURT, and we are correct.

HERRING-GOLDFISH-HADDOCK

PLAYERS: *two to four*
LOCATION: *anywhere*
EQUIPMENT: *none*
SPECIAL SKILL: *vocabulary*

This clever word game goes by at least a dozen names and rule variations. The game is most often played by two, but any number can participate. There is no equipment or action involved, and you can play it anywhere. This is not a game for young players.

First, select a category—any category, such as cities, animals, or famous people, so long as it is not too specific. Now select a player to go first. This player calls out any object he likes that belongs to the category. For example, if the category were fish, he might call out, "Herring."

The next player must call out another object belonging to the category, and it must start with the last letter of the previous object. In our example of "herring," the next player would have to name a fish beginning with the letter *g,* such as "goldfish." The next player then must name a fish beginning with the letter *h,* the last letter in "goldfish."

If a player hesitates too long or calls out an object that does not belong to the current category or does not begin with the correct letter, that player is out of the game. Play continues until there is only one player left, who is declared the winner.

To make the game playable and fun for young children, don't place the restriction of categories on the game. Let the children name *any* word beginning with the last letter of the previous one.

CATEGORIES

PLAYERS: *any number*
LOCATION: *anywhere*
EQUIPMENT: *pencils and paper*
SPECIAL SKILLS: *memory, trivia*

CATEGORIES, also known by the name Guggenheim, is another classic American word game whose origins have become obscured. It is designed for any number of players, requires only pencils and paper, and tests your powers of trivia and association to the maximum. It's a great rainy-day pastime for a group of bored people.

First, distribute a pencil and a piece of paper to each player; have each draw the figure in Diagram 5.2, without the labels. To set up the categories for the game, each player is allowed to make nominations that the rest of the group vote on. Categories can be general or specific, such as Rock 'n' Roll Bands, Vegetables, Actors, Countries, Magazines, and so forth. Caution: don't use a category that is too specific, such as Eighteenth-Century Violin Makers; otherwise players will not be able to think of *anything* that fits the category.

Diagram 5.2   CATEGORIES

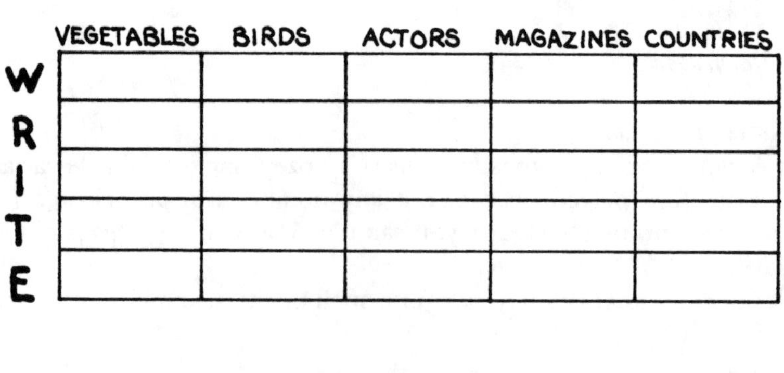

	VEGETABLES	BIRDS	ACTORS	MAGAZINES	COUNTRIES
W					
R					
I					
T					
E					

Once you have decided on five categories, each player should list them along the top of the grid as shown on the top of Diagram 5.3. Now the group must decide on a key word of five letters in length—something like "opera," "grand," or "flame"—a word that does not repeat any letters. In our diagram, we're using the word "write." You might also try to pick a word *without* uncommon letters such as *q* or *z,* as those will make the game much more difficult.

Diagram 5.3

	VEGETABLES	BIRDS	ACTORS	MAGAZINES	COUNTRIES
W		wren	Eli Wallach	Writer's Digest	
R		robin	Robert Redford	Reader's Digest	Rumania
I		ibis			Iraq
T	Turnip	Tern	Tom Tryon	Tennis	Tunisia
E		eagle	Chad Everett	Ebony	Ecuador

Once you have decided on the five-letter key word, each player should write the letters down the left side of the grid as shown. Agree upon a time limit of five, ten, or fifteen minutes, then start the game. Players must try to fill in the blanks in the categories with names that start with the letters along the left side of the grid.

When the time limit is reached, scoring begins. There are two methods. The first is simply to give each player one point for each box he has filled in with a valid name. Under the second method you would first cross out words that all players had in common. Then you count the occurrence of each player's entries. If there are five players in the game and four have the same word in a box, that word is worth one point. (Subtract the number of players who got the word from the number of players.) If there are five players, but only two got the word, it is worth three points. An adult might be necessary to perform the scoring in this manner.

The legality of all words is decided by democratic voting among the players.

For the next round, you may use the same categories with a different key word, the same key word with different categories, or a new key word and categories.

ADVERBS

PLAYERS: *any number*
LOCATION: *anywhere*
EQUIPMENT: *none*
SPECIAL SKILLS: *acting, vocabulary*

ADVERBS is a classic word-guessing game that includes some of the theatrics of CHARADES, and it is easy to modify the game for any skill level or age range of players. No equipment is required.

First, select one player to be It, and send It out of the room. Next, agree on an adverb that It must guess. Easy adverbs might be "slowly," "happily," and "secretly." More difficult would be "persistently," "willfully," and "abnormally." Nearly impossible would be "moderately," "personably," and "handily." Choose something neither too difficult nor too easy for It to guess.

Having settled on an adverb among the group, invite It back into the room and begin the round. It may turn to any player and ask that player to perform some act in the manner of the adverb. For example, I might say "Chris, shake hands with Tom in the manner of the adverb." If the adverb in this case was "vigorously," Chris would go over to Tom and shake his hand vigorously.

The player who is It alternates guesses at the adverb with requests of the other players for more clues. Players may not speak during their acting, so It should not ask them to do so. Actions, alone, are meant to convey the adverb.

Play continues until the adverb has been guessed or until It gives up in frustration. At this point, the last player requested to perform an act becomes the new It for the next round of play.

TELEGRAMS

PLAYERS: *any number*
LOCATION: *anywhere*
EQUIPMENT: *pencils and paper*
SPECIAL SKILLS: *creativity, vocabulary*

This pencil-and-paper game for three or more players is designed to stimulate creativity, originality, and humor, at any skill level. The only requirement for playing TELEGRAMS is the ability to read and write. Oddly enough, despite the silliness of the intentions of TELEGRAMS, it appeals to *all* age groups.

Give each player a pencil and a piece of paper and arrange everyone comfortably so that no one can see his neighbor's paper. Decide who will go first, and establish an order of play for everyone else.

Now each player in turn calls out a letter of the alphabet and everyone writes them down across the top of the paper. Continue calling out letters until the players have either five, ten, or fifteen letters, depending on how difficult you wish to make the game. Use five letters for an easier game; fifteen for a much more difficult one.

Give the players a time limit of five minutes (you may shorten or lengthen this) to create a telegram out of the letters. You do this by using each letter as the first letter of a word. Example: let's say the letters are *h, a, r, w, t, e, b, f, i, c.* My telegram might read: "**H**aving **A R**eally **W**eird **T**ime **E**ating **B**ananas **F**ried **I**n **C**hocolate."

Get the idea? After the time limit is up, each player reads his telegram aloud. Declare the owner of the most original, cleverest, funniest telegram the winner.

CROSSWORDS

PLAYERS: *any number*
LOCATION: *anywhere*
EQUIPMENT: *pencils and paper*
SPECIAL SKILL: *word building*

Whether or not you enjoy solving crossword puzzles has no bearing on your enjoyment of this wonderful paper-and-pencil word game for two or more players. It is an ingenious diversion for long car rides and other boring situations in which people are not free to move about. Just leave the driver out of this one!

First, give each player a sheet of paper and a pencil to draw identical blank grids of 5 × 5 squares. If there are more than four or five players, you may construct a slightly larger grid, say 6 × 6 or 7 × 7. Also, increase the size of the grid for lengthier games.

Next, establish who will go first and the order of play for everyone else. In turn, each player calls out one letter of the alphabet, and all players must enter it somewhere within their grids. It does not matter in which square you enter a letter, but keep in mind that the object of the game is to form as many legal words as possible. So don't put any qs or zs in the middle!

The game continues with players alternately calling out letters of their choosing until the grids are full. Then scoring begins. Words must be at least three letters long to qualify, and they must be found in the dictionary, whatever one you have in your house. Score three points for each three-letter word, four points for each four-letter word (subtract four points for any dirty four-letter words!), and so on. If a word is contained within a longer one, only the longer one is scored. Words must be spelled from left to right or from top to bottom of the grid. Diagram 5.4 shows two completely filled-in grids and how each would be scored.

The winner is the player with the highest score.

GHOST

PLAYERS: *two to four*
LOCATION: *anywhere*
EQUIPMENT: *none*
SPECIAL SKILL: *vocabulary*

GHOST is a very clever word game for older children and adults—not because it's scary, but because you need solid word-building skills to have fun. One of the beauties of GHOST is that the game is spoken aloud, so there is no equipment or special play area necessary. You may play in the living room, in the car, canoeing down a river, or wherever you happen to be with at least one other player.

You don't want too many players for GHOST, because each player won't get enough turns per round to make the game interesting. Four players is probably a

Diagram 5.4   CROSSWORDS

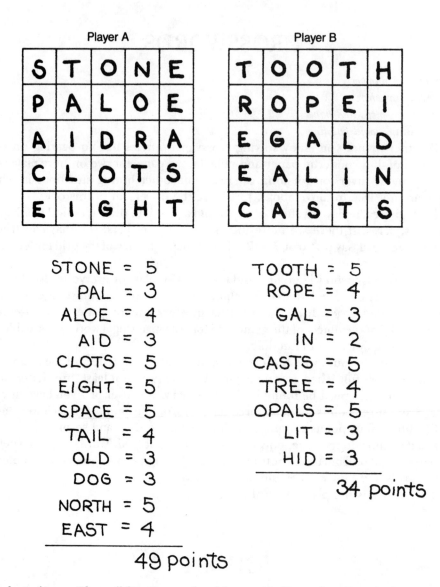

Player A

S	T	O	N	E
P	A	L	O	E
A	I	D	R	A
C	L	O	T	S
E	I	G	H	T

Player B

T	O	O	T	H
R	O	P	E	I
E	G	A	L	D
E	A	L	I	N
C	A	S	T	S

STONE = 5
PAL = 3
ALOE = 4
AID = 3
CLOTS = 5
EIGHT = 5
SPACE = 5
TAIL = 4
OLD = 3
DOG = 3
NORTH = 5
EAST = 4

49 points

TOOTH = 5
ROPE = 4
GAL = 3
IN = 2
CASTS = 5
TREE = 4
OPALS = 5
LIT = 3
HID = 3

34 points

good maximum. If possible, players should arrange themselves in a circle so that the order of play is visibly obvious.

The object of the game is for players to create a lengthening chain of letters without forming any legal words. Anyone may go first by calling out a letter of the alphabet. The next player must add a letter to the first so that it does *not* complete a legal word, while making the other players think he has a word in mind. The following example will clear this up:

The first player says, "T," thinking of any word that begins with that letter. The second player adds an *a*, thinking of the word "talon." A third player adds an *l*, thinking of the word "talent."

As players add letters and the chain grows longer, it becomes more difficult to add a new letter to the chain that doesn't form a legal word. Also, any player's new letter may be challenged by any other player. To continue the example above, let's say the next player adds an *f* to the chain, making it "talf." Another player would likely challenge the *f,* thinking that there are no words beginning with those letters. The challenged player must either give a legal word beginning with talf, or become a ghost and drop out of the game.

If a player adds a letter that forms a legal word, another player may challenge. The word is looked up in the dictionary, and the loser of the challenge becomes a ghost by dropping out of the game.

A player may not hesitate long when it comes his turn to add a letter. Of course, bluffing is as much a part of GHOST as it is of poker. There is nothing wrong with adding a letter that forms a legal word or one that could not possibly lead to any word, so long as it slips past the other players unchallenged.

I SPY

PLAYERS: *any number*
LOCATION: *anywhere*
EQUIPMENT: *none*
SPECIAL SKILL: *visual searching*

This simple game is subtle and easy enough to captivate the interest of children and young teenagers who don't want a game that's difficult to learn or remember. It is entirely verbal, so nothing except your surroundings is required. And the beauty of I SPY is that it works equally well in any environment, from the living room to the campground to the car. In fact, the more boring the current environment the more enjoyment the game brings.

There is no set beginning or end to I SPY, nor is there any order of play. One player simply starts the ball rolling by locating some identifiable object in plain sight of all other players and announcing, "I spy with my little eye something beginning with the letter __," filling in the blank with the first letter of the object he has in mind.

The rest of the players begin searching the room and announcing objects that begin with that letter as the possible answer. "Is it a _____?" they ask. The answer can be only "Yes" or "No." The first player to correctly guess the object gets to announce the next one.

To illustrate, I might look around, see a thumbtack on a bulletin board and say, "I spy with my little eye something that begins with the letter *t.*" The other players would then guess until one found the thumbtack.

Obviously, you should not choose a housefly or a bird or a dog that is likely to wander out of sight during the game!

PAIRING OFF

PLAYERS: *any number*
LOCATION: *anywhere*
EQUIPMENT: *index cards, tape, pencil*
SPECIAL SKILLS: *deduction, sleuthing*

The point of this game is to break the ice at a party or large children's gathering, and it requires a little preparation work on the part of the host. Players should know nothing of the game in advance and should become part of it on arrival.

Before anyone arrives, prepare a stack of index cards. Each card should bear the name of one member of a famous couple, and you should have as many cards as you have players. In case you get an odd number of players, prepare three cards with the names of members of a famous trio.

For example, if you're having ten players, you might prepare cards for Martha Washington and George Washington, George Burns and Gracie Allen, Anthony and Cleopatra, Marie Osmond and Donny Osmond. As each guest arrives, select a card at random and pin it or tape it to his back without his reading the name.

The object of the game is to be the first player to locate its "other half." George and Martha Washington would be looking for one another; so would Anthony and Cleopatra; and so forth. Unfortunately, players don't know who they are looking for, because they don't know who they *are!* So each player should set out to discover himself by asking questions of the other players. Anything is fair except a question such as "Who am I?" The other players are allowed to look at the name tag and give hints or answers to the identities, but only in response to direct questions.

If you play with a group of young children, use famous couples from cartoons, comic books, and so forth, like Batman and Robin, or Tom Sawyer and Huck Finn.

Caution: Remove all mirrors from the playing room.

CHAPTER SIX
Number and Dice Games

Many games involving numbers and/or dice are too difficult, too complicated, or not exciting enough to maintain the interest of children. Most gambling games are guilty of this. But the nine games presented in the following pages are all enjoyable by children.

A side benefit of these games is their focus on numbers, counting, arithmetic, and mathematical probability. The games, indeed, are instructive and beneficial to children. I have selected these games also for their "fun quotient," because children will stay with a fun game no matter how taxing it may be on their minds.

Other than dice, counters, pencils, and paper, there is no equipment required for these games. They travel nearly as well as word games.

NIM

PLAYERS: *two*
LOCATION: *anywhere*
EQUIPMENT: *matchsticks, pebbles, or coins*
SPECIAL SKILLS: *counting, planning*

NIM is an ancient arithmetic challenge for two players that originated in China as an intellectual pursuit. It was named NIM in 1901 by Charles Bouton, a Harvard professor of mathematics who became fascinated with numerical and mathematical games. NIM may be played anywhere, anytime, and almost anything may be improvised for playing pieces. Countless variations on NIM have developed over the centuries, and the game is found in nearly every culture, under various names.

Rows of coins (or pebbles or sticks) are laid on the ground or table, with a specific arrangement, to form the playing board. Diagram 6.1 shows three kinds of arrangement; many other starting formations exist.

Select the order of play. Then each player in turn is allowed to remove any number of coins or pebbles from any single row. You may take one, several, or all of the objects from any row on your turn. The winner is the player who is able to force his opponent to have the last turn and pick up the last coin or pebble.

That's all there is to it.

In one variation of the game, the objects are laid out in a single row, usually fifteen, twenty-one, or twenty-five objects. Then each player in turn is allowed to remove one, two, or three objects from the board. Again, the player who must pick up the last object is the loser.

In another variation, objects are laid out in a rectangular grid. Then each player

Diagram 6.1   NIM: COIN LAYOUTS

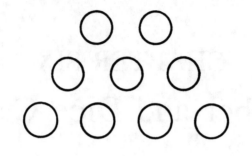

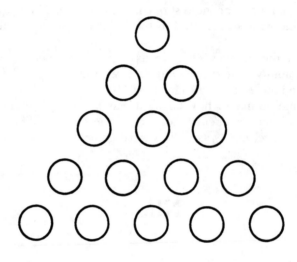

Diagram 6.2 NIM: PLAYING BOARD

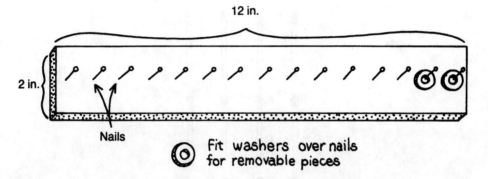

in turn is allowed to remove one or two objects. If he removes two, they must be touching. The winner of this variation is the player who picks up the last object.

TAC TIX

PLAYERS: *two*
LOCATION: *anywhere*
EQUIPMENT: *matchsticks*
SPECIAL SKILLS: *counting, planning*

The Danish mathematician Piet Hein is also the inventor of this intriguing two-player matchstick game and several popular board strategy games. You will recognize in TAC TIX similarities to variations of NIM, but none are as elegant or as strategically complex as the innocent-looking TAC TIX board.

The game is formed on a table or the ground using sixteen sticks arranged in four rows and four columns as shown in Diagram 6.3. Players should agree who will go first. The first player removes any number of sticks from any column or row, so long as the sticks are adjacent. The second player does the same, removing one, two, three, or four sticks from any row or column. Again, the sticks must be adjacent.

The winner of the game, as in NIM, is the player who forces his opponent to remove the last stick from the board. The game may also be played using twenty-five or thirty-six sticks in a 5 × 5 or a 6 × 6 grid.

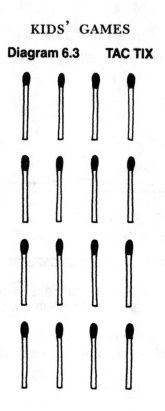

Diagram 6.3   TAC TIX

ARITHMETIC CROQUET

PLAYERS: *two*

LOCATION: *anywhere*

EQUIPMENT: *paper and pencil*

SPECIAL SKILLS: *arithmetic, planning*

Lewis Carroll became a much more famous and recognized personality for works such as *Alice in Wonderland* than did Charles Dodgson for his brilliant work in the field of mathematics. Yet both names belonged to the same man. Carroll (or Dodgson if you prefer) was also an incessant game and puzzle inventor, largely for the amusement of the children he knew and loved. Most of his games involved mathematics, language, or deductive reasoning.

ARITHMETIC CROQUET is an amusing paper-and-pencil variation of the sport that Alice had found so intriguing on the lawns of Wonderland. The game is for two players who will have no trouble adding and subtracting numbers up to one hundred. The game is ideal for an adult who wishes to teach or improve arithmetic abilities in a child.

Most of us are not quite as adept as Carroll at arithmetic, so I don't suggest scoring the game in your head, as he would do. Use a pencil and a piece of paper. Draw a series of "wickets" down the center of the page as shown in Diagram 6.4, labeling them, by tens, 10 through 100. On either side of the wickets, create columns for the scores headed by each player's name.

Decide who will go first. The first player chooses a number from one through eight and writes it down in the column beneath his name. Now the second player takes

Diagram 6.4   ARITHMETIC CROQUET

Player A's score	Player B's score

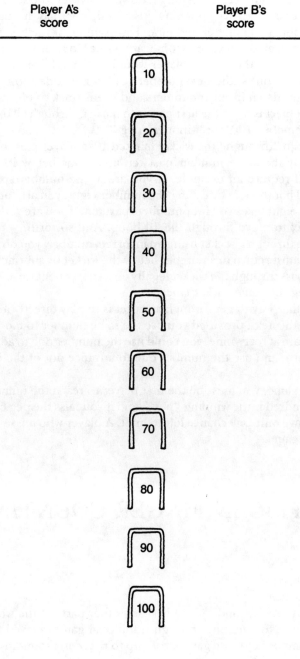

a turn by choosing a number and writing it down. However, the second player may *not* use the same number as his opponent just used, nor may he use the difference between the opponent's number and nine. For example, if the first player used four, the second player would be barred from using either four or five on that turn. If the first player used seven, the second player would be barred from using seven or two.

On subsequent turns, the new numbers called are added to the previous ones. Each player writes down his own numbers and keeps track of his own score through the hoops. The object is to be the first player to make it through all the hoops, landing exactly on the number 100, the winning "peg."

In order to go "through" the wicket marked 10, a player must use a number that takes him exactly the same number past ten as he was below it. This is a simple concept but will require an example. If you are at the number six, you may move through the "10 hoop" only by calling the number eight: you are four away from ten, and the number eight takes you four numbers past ten. If you are at the number seven, you must use six to move through the 10 hoop. And so forth.

If you move through a wicket using an incorrect number, you do not get credit for the wicket. You must return to a number below the wicket by subtracting on your next turn and try to pass through the wicket legally on a subsequent turn. A player loses the game by missing the same wicket twice.

The only other way to get through a wicket is to play directly into it on one turn and out of it on the next, provided you use the same number to move in and out. For example, if you are at forty-nine, you could use the number one to advance into the 50 hoop on one turn, and use the number one to advance out of the 50 hoop on your next turn.

To win the game, you must be the first player to reach the number one hundred exactly. One hundred is the winning "peg," and if you miss the peg by going over one hundred, you have only one chance left to hit it. A player who misses the winning peg twice loses the game.

AFRICAN FINGER COUNTING

PLAYERS: *any number*
LOCATION: *anywhere*
EQUIPMENT: *your fingers*
SPECIAL SKILL: *counting*

In all parts of Africa, and indeed in many other parts of the world, children get their first exposure to counting through traditional games played with rhymes and rhythms. The simplest of these games goes up to five, corresponding to the fingers of one hand. Others continue to ten, using the other hand, and twenty, using both fingers and toes. These games, with their thousands of local variations, entrance even those children who don't yet know their numbers.

Finger-counting games can be played using traditional rhymes and verses, but children find the game most enjoyable when played with familiar ones, such as:

> One, two, buckle my shoe.
> Three, four, out the door.
> Five, six, pick up sticks.

> Seven, eight, don't be late.
> Nine, ten, a big fat hen!

Children are shown how to begin with their fingers clenched in fists, stretching out one finger with the count of each number in the rhyme. Here's another:

> One little, two little, three little Indians,
> Four little, five little, six little Indians,
> Seven little, eight little, nine little Indians,
> Ten little Indian boys.

AFRICAN FINGER COUNTING is also played during the recital of familiar poems. Children are encouraged to count out one finger for each beat of the poem, with everyone looking around to see who's missed a beat. Try this game using ten fingers over and over again to a recitation of *The Midnight Ride of Paul Revere* or *The Charge of the Light Brigade.*

WARI

PLAYERS: *two*
LOCATION: *table or floor*
EQUIPMENT: *playing board, forty-eight counters*
SPECIAL SKILLS: *counting, addition, planning*

African children progress from the FINGER COUNTING games of childhood to the WARI board of youth, which is traditionally either carved of wood or molded of clay, or sculptured into the earth wherever two African players happen to be. Playing pieces are pebbles found anywhere. Thus, its popularity spans the gap between nobility and peasant. The game of WARI belongs to a group of African number games called *mancala,* or pit-and-pebble games, and they are thousands of years old. The exact origin is lost, but over the centuries variations have been spread throughout Africa, Syria, Indonesia, the Philippines, Malaysia, South America, and the Carribean islands, where they are actively played today.

WARI is the African version of *mancala,* but there are even dozens of tribal variations on WARI. The rules presented below are based on one of the most commonly played and most fun variations. These games are for two players at a time.

You probably won't want to dig pits in your backyard to play WARI, so you'll have to make or improvise a board. See Diagram 6.5. Several years ago I made one in five minutes. I bought a nice, rectangular piece of wood, about two inches thick, borrowed someone's drill press, used a rounded one-inch drill bit, and sculptured the twelve playing pits. I then glued a small ceramic cup on each end.

However, there's a much easier way to get started. Use an empty egg carton for the main playing board and place a cup at each end. Playing pieces are traditionally pebbles, but you could use beans, buttons, whatever you have handy in quantity. You'll need forty-eight of these counters; it doesn't matter what color or if they are assorted colors. A friend and I used to play with little metal BBs years ago, picking them up from the holes with a magnet.

To begin the basic game, players sit on opposite sides of the board and distribute four pebbles (or whatever) into each of the twelve pits as shown in Diagram 6.6. This

Diagram 6.5   WARI: PLAYING BOARD

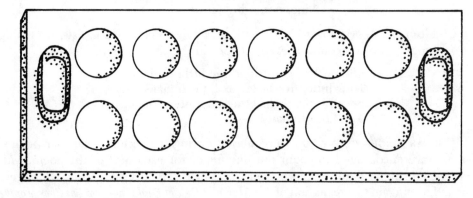

is the opening position. No pebbles are in the scoring cups at either end of the board yet. Players should decide whose cup is whose, and who shall go first.

The first player picks up all the pebbles from any pit on his side of the board and drops them one by one into the next pits in a counterclockwise direction. The twelve

Diagram 6.6   WARI: STARTING POSITION

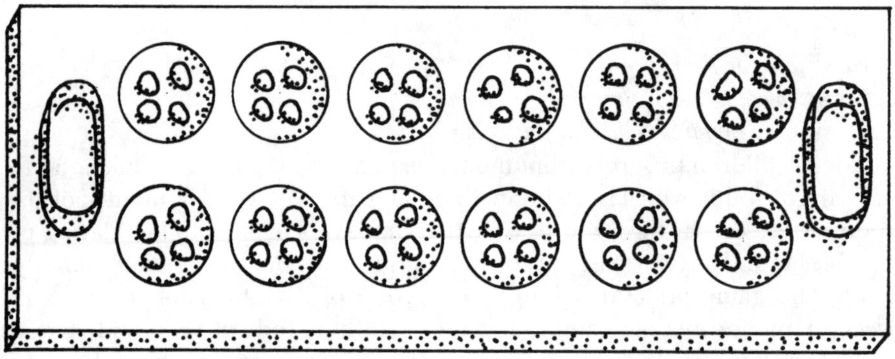

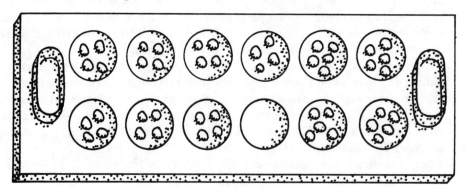

pits in the board are connected in an oval. For example, in Diagram 6.7, the first player has picked up all four pebbles from one of his pits and placed one of them in each of the next four pits, moving around the board to his right and into the pits on his opponent's side of the board. This is known as "sowing the pebbles." Pebbles are not dropped into either cup at the end of the board.

Diagram 6.7   WARI: AFTER ONE MOVE

When sewing pebbles, the only rule is that a player must take *all* the pebbles from one of the six pits on *his* side of the board.

If a player's last pebble lands in a pit on the opponent's side of the board and creates a minimum of two pebbles in that pit, those pebbles are captured by the current player and placed in his scoring cup at the end of the board. This ends the player's turn. Captured pebbles are never reentered into play.

Players alternate turns in this manner, taking pebbles from pits on their own sides of the board and sowing them into subsequent holes. After a while, there might be twelve or more pebbles in a single pit. When a player sows enough pebbles to make it all the way around the board, he must skip the original pit.

If it is your turn to move, but all pits on your opponent's side of the board are empty, you *must* make a move that places pebbles on his side if you can. Otherwise, the game ends. The game also ends when one player has made the last move possible. The player with the greatest number of pebbles in his scoring cup is the winner.

BEETLE

PLAYERS: *two to six*
LOCATION: *table or floor*
EQUIPMENT: *paper, pencils, pair of dice*
SPECIAL SKILL: *none*

BEETLE, also known by the name Cootie, is the most amusing dice game I know of for young children. (My four-year-old son enjoys it.) It may be played by any number, though more than five or six won't produce as much fun as will a smaller group. The necessary equipment is a pair of dice, a pad of paper, and some pencils.

First, establish the order in which players will take turns by rolling the dice—highest roll goes first—and give each player a piece of paper and a pencil. In turn, each player rolls the dice once. The six possibilities on each die represent parts of the beetle as follows:

1	=	the body
2	=	the head
3	=	one leg
4	=	one eye
5	=	one feeler
6	=	the tail

The object of the game is to throw numbers that allow you to add parts to your beetle and be the first player to finish. As shown by Diagram 6.8, a complete beetle has thirteen parts to it—the body, the head, two eyes, two feelers, six legs, and the tail—so, to win, a player must roll one 1, one 2, six 3s, two 4s, two 5s, and one 6.

To make matters a little more difficult, there is one additional rule: no player may begin drawing beetle parts until he has a beetle's *body* on which to draw them. Therefore, each player must roll a 1 and draw the body before he may use a roll of 2, 3, 4, 5, or 6 to add the other parts.

When a player rolls one or two numbers that he needs, he adds the corresponding part or parts to his beetle. The winner is the first player to complete his drawing of the beetle.

Diagram 6.8   BEETLE

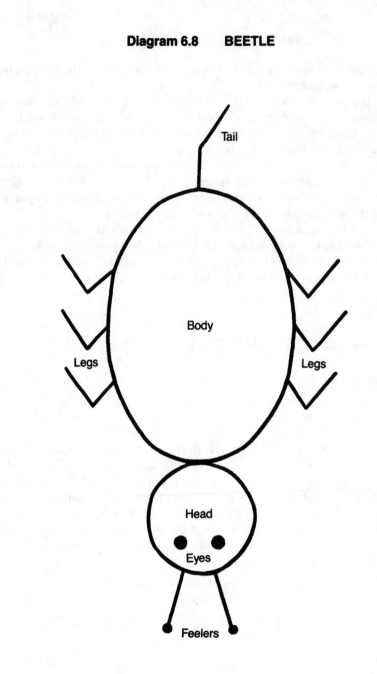

GOING TO BOSTON

PLAYERS: *two or more*
LOCATION: *table or floor*
EQUIPMENT: *three dice*
SPECIAL SKILL: *none*

No one seems to remember the reason for the name of this classic dice game. Perhaps its inventor played it on the train while commuting into Boston. It is as reasonable an explanation as any. The game is played by two or more players and requires three dice.

Decide who will go first and establish an order of play. The first player rolls the three dice, then takes the die with the highest number and places it to the side. If the high number shows on two dice, only one is removed. He now rolls just the two remaining dice, again placing the one with the higher number to the side. Finally, he rolls the third die. His score is the total of the three dice.

Play continues in this manner until all players have had a turn. The player with the highest score wins. Usually, players keep score on paper over an agreed-upon number of rounds.

SHUT THE BOX

PLAYERS: *two or more*
LOCATION: *table or floor*
EQUIPMENT: *playing board, two dice, nine counters*
SPECIAL SKILLS: *addition, planning*

This is a very popular French game of chance for two or more players that is played traditionally on a special board. It would not be difficult to create your own wooden board, but you may also draw it on a piece of paper. You will need two dice and nine counters such as pennies.

First, draw the board, which is actually just nine squares containing the numbers 1 through 9. Place the pennies just above the numbers as shown in Diagram 6.9. Then establish an order of play.

The object for each player in turn is to roll numbers with the dice that allow him to cover as many numbers as possible on the board. Each player begins each turn with *none* of the nine numbers covered by pennies.

A player throws the pair of dice and adds their numbers together. He must now look to the board for two *uncovered* numbers that total his dice roll and cover those numbers with pennies. For example, if the first player rolled a 5 and a 4, for a total of nine, he would be allowed to cover the 8 and the 1, the 7 and the 2, the 6 and the 3, or the 5 and the 4. He would also be allowed to choose and cover three numbers that total nine, such as the 1, the 2, and the 6. The choice of which numbers to cover is always up to the player.

The player rolls the dice again, this time trying to cover the remaining numbers

Diagram 6.9   SHUT THE BOX

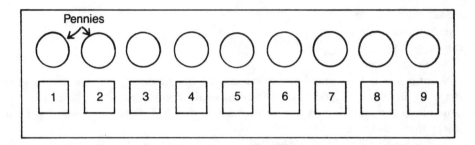

on the board. The player continues taking turns until he cannot find a combination of numbers on the board that totals the numbers he has thrown on the dice. This ends his turn. The remaining *uncovered* numbers are totaled, forming the player's score for that turn.

The game continues until all players have had a turn. The player with the *lowest* score at the end of the game is the winner.

YACHT

PLAYERS: *any number*
LOCATION: *table or floor*
EQUIPMENT: *five dice, cup, paper, and pencil*
SPECIAL SKILL: *planning*

YACHT is a very old game of chance and popular with children and adults alike. There are dozens of variations on the name and the rules; below, I describe the most common variation. Although the game does not require complex skills to play, young children may need an adult to do the scoring. Any number can play, and it is well suited for family play, accommodating a wide range of ages. To play, you'll need five dice, a throwing cup, and paper and pencil for scoring.

First, establish an order of play around the table. To help players remember the twelve types of scoring combinations, leave this book open within everyone's sight. On each turn, a player must select one of the scoring combinations and try to throw numbers to gain the highest possible score. A player may select each combination only once during the game. Therefore, a game consists of twelve rounds, or turns, and all players will try each scoring combination once.

To begin a turn, a player rolls all five dice from the throwing cup. The player may let all five dice stand and score their values, or he may take back as many dice as he wishes and reroll them. The player may reroll any of the dice a third time. Thus, on each turn, a player may roll the dice three times, trying to get the numbers he needs.

Using a paper scorepad as shown in Diagram 6.10, the player's score is recorded in the proper row by the following rules:

Diagram 6.10   YACHT

	Player 1	Player 2	Player 3	Player 4
Aces				
Twos				
Threes				
Fours				
Fives				
Sixes				
Little straight				
Big straight				
Full house				
Four of a kind				
Choice				
Yacht				
Final scores				

	NAME	MAXIMUMS
1)	Yacht	50 points
2)	Big straight	30 points
3)	Little straight	30 points
4)	Four of a kind	29 points
5)	Full house	28 points
6)	Choice	30 points
7)	Sixes	30 points
8)	Fives	25 points
9)	Fours	20 points
10)	Threes	15 points
11)	Twos	10 points
12)	Aces	5 points

Scoring is not as simple as it seems, but that's what makes the game interesting. Below are some examples that illustrate how to score the twelve combinations.

1) Yacht: this is five of a kind, such as five 3s or five 6s. The maximum score is 50 points.
2) Big straight: this is a 2, 3, 4, 5, and 6.
3) Little straight: this is a 1, 2, 3, 4, and 5.
4) Four of a kind: this scores to total number of spots on the five dice, regardless of whether or not there are actually four of a kind. Twenty-nine points is the maximum.
5) Full house: this is three of a kind plus two of another kind, such as three 2s and two 5s. A full house scores the total number of spots on the five dice, regardless of whether or not the player actually has three of a kind plus two of another kind. Twenty-eight points is the maximum.

6) Choice: there is no pattern to choice. It scores the value of the five dice added together. Thirty points is the maximum.

7–12) Sixes, fives, fours, threes, twos, and aces score similarly. As an example, sixes would score six times the number of 6s thrown, for a maximum of thirty points. Thus, two 6s scores twelve points; three 6s scores eighteen points; and so on. Fives would score five times the number of 5s thrown. Thus, two 5s scores ten points; three 5s scores fifteen.

As you can tell, there is a lot of flexibility to the game. Players may select a scoring combination after they have rolled all the dice, and this is where the strategy comes in: pick your scoring combinations carefully, and don't leave the hardest ones for last. Remember: you must try to score for each of the twelve combinations during the game. It is possible to score 0 on a turn if you have few combinations left and none of your dice fit them.

At the end of the twelve rounds of play, the player with the highest total score wins.

CHAPTER SEVEN
Memory and Guessing Games

The games in this chapter emphasize and exercise the skills of memory and intuition with amusing challenges that delight children of all ages. Memory is one of the most important faculties a child has in his favor in understanding the world at large, and if we can stimulate and develop this in children while providing safe, healthful, and exciting recreation, nature will do the rest.

Memory and guessing games come in many forms, and the selections described below are quite varied, so that every age, skill, and interest level is served. No matter the object, all the games in this chapter place a premium on having fun. Although some of the games require physical activity, none demand physical skills. Their purpose is to get children to stretch upward on the tiptoes of their minds.

BLIND MAN'S BUFF

PLAYERS: *five or more*
LOCATION: *anywhere*
EQUIPMENT: *blindfold*
SPECIAL SKILL: *none*

BLIND MAN'S BUFF, often mistakenly called BLIND MAN'S BLUFF, is an old favorite with young children, though older players enjoy the game too. You'll need at least five or six players to make the game any fun, and it can be played anywhere, with only a handkerchief or a small towel for equipment.

First, select one player to be the first blind man, and tie a blindfold around his head. The other players join hands in a circle around the blind man and begin to dance in one direction, chanting whatever they like. ("Three Blind Mice" might be appropriate!) In any case, all must sing or chant loudly enough so that the blind man hears verbal clues as to the players' whereabouts in the moving circle.

When the blind man calls out, "Stop!" the ring of players comes to a halt and the blind man points in the direction of his choice. The player he is pointing nearest to must let go of the others and enter the circle, quietly, until he is facing the blind man within arm's reach. The player might shuffle his feet at this point to signify that he is there.

The blind man must now catch the player, who is free to duck and move away amid the laughter of the others. But he may not leave the circle, so sooner or later it is inevitable that he will be caught. Now the blind man tries to guess which player stands before him by feeling only the player's face and head. If correct, the blind man exchanges the blindfold with the other player and joins the circle for the next round. If incorrect, he must try the whole thing again.

PIN THE TAIL ON THE DONKEY

PLAYERS: *any number*
LOCATION: *anywhere you can hang the picture*
EQUIPMENT: *large sheet of paper, marker, pushpin, string*
SPECIAL SKILL: *none*

This amusing game of luck is great for gatherings of young children who haven't the patience to compete with their skills. A funny game of chance like PIN THE TAIL ON THE DONKEY is perfect for those moments.

Of course, the game does take a bit of advance preparation. Using a large sheet of paper, even newspaper, draw the outline of a donkey as best you can, but leave out the donkey's tail. Hang the sheet of paper on a wall or tree at about shoulder height for the children. Then attach about a dozen one-foot lengths of string to the pushpin, making a donkey's tail.

Line up the players about three or four feet in front of the picture of the donkey. In turn, a player is blindfolded, spun around slowly three times, then faced directly toward the donkey. The player must walk forward, tail pushpin held point out, until he comes in contact with the wall. Then the pin is pushed into the wall and the player may remove the blindfold. This spot on the donkey, or the paper, is marked with the player's name or initials. Then the next player goes.

The winner of the game is the player who came closest to pinning the tail where the donkey's tail should be.

SQUEAL, PIGGY, SQUEAL!

PLAYERS: *six or more*
LOCATION: *anywhere*
EQUIPMENT: *blindfold*
SPECIAL SKILL: *none*

This is a wonderfully funny game; whoever devised it must have a great sense of humor. I'd like to have him at our next party. Anyway, the game is played much like BLIND MAN'S BUFF.

First, select the first blind man, and blindfold him. Arm the blind man with a small seat cushion or pillow. The other players should join hands in a circle and dance in one direction, singing or chanting anything that comes to mind. When the blind man calls, "Stop!" everyone must stop. The blind man then points in any direction, and the nearest player must enter the circle and sit cross-legged on the floor.

The blind man now places the cushion in the player's lap and sits on it, commanding the player to give him a clue, by saying, "Squeal, piggy, squeal!" The player on whom he is sitting must then squeal like a pig, just once. Now the blind man guesses which player he is sitting on. If correct, they exchange roles. If incorrect, the game starts again with the same blind man.

INDIAN

PLAYERS: *two or more*
LOCATION: *table or floor*
EQUIPMENT: *deck of cards, counters*
SPECIAL SKILL: *observation*

INDIAN is a silly American game whose origin was lost in some college fraternity dorm many years ago, but which has been passed on by word of mouth ever since. It is a pleasant diversion from more serious competitions. The only equipment required is a deck of cards and some counters for each player.

Two can play, but more is merrier. One player acts as the dealer, shuffling a deck of cards. (INDIAN is *not* classified as a card game despite the fact that it uses cards.) The dealer has a choice of calling, "High" or "Low," before he deals one card to each player. High simply means that the highest-ranking card will win the round; low, the opposite. Ace is higher than king in this game.

Players must pick up their cards and hold them to their foreheads without looking at their own cards. In this manner, you will be able to see the value of everyone's card except your own. Beginning with the dealer, each player may bet any number of counters (based on a predetermined limit) that he holds the highest card. You may raise another player's bet, call it (equal it), or fold your hand.

Play continues until no one can stand the silliness any longer. The only skill applicable to INDIAN is the ability to read other people's faces.

GRANDMOTHER'S TRUNK

PLAYERS: *three or more*
LOCATION: *anywhere*
EQUIPMENT: *none*
SPECIAL SKILL: *memory*

This excellent memory-testing game has been played by generations of American families as a subtle way of parents' encouraging the development of their children's minds. Not to worry, though, because children of all ages love the game, particularly if you place no restrictions on their imaginations. By the way, you may know this game under another name such as I Went on a Trip, or I Packed My Bag, or some such name. I am sure there are dozens of variations on the name, but the theme is always the same: to remember an ever-lengthening set of items.

You need at least three people for a good game of GRANDMOTHER'S TRUNK, more if you have them, but limit the group to not more than eight or ten. No equipment or special play area is needed.

First, decide who will start, and establish a playing order for everyone else. The first player thinks of something, a radio, for example, and says, "I put a radio in

Grandmother's trunk." The next player must think of another object, a bar of soap, for example, and add it by saying, "I put a radio and a bar of soap in Grandmother's trunk."

In this manner, the sentence gets longer and longer and longer until players begin to forget everything that has been packed in Grandmother's trunk. When a player makes a mistake reciting the sentence, he is disqualified, and play continues. The last player remaining is the winner and gets to start a new round.

A more difficult variation of the game requires that the objects be loaded into Grandmother's trunk *alphabetically!* A partially constructed sentence would read something like this: "I put an antler, a biscuit, a canary, a dodo bird, and an Eastern 747 Jumbo Jet in Grandmother's trunk." There is no restriction on how long an entry may be, so long as it starts with the next letter of the alphabet. Of course, the group can always object and veto one that is too long or too difficult to remember.

TIBETAN MEMORY TRICK

PLAYERS: *two or more*
LOCATION: *anywhere*
EQUIPMENT: *this book*
SPECIAL SKILL: *memory*

There isn't the slightest clue as to the origin of this memory game, so we shall fantasize that it was devised to challenge the sharpest minds of Eastern mystics, somewhere in the mountains of Tibet, hundreds of years ago. In any case, it is also a terrific party game for a large group of people who think they're so smart! The TIBETAN MEMORY TRICK is no trick, just good memory. And it's guaranteed for laughs.

You don't need any equipment to play the game except this book or a copy of the list of phrases below, or someone who can actually remember them all! And any number can play in turn. You might make up an easier, shorter set of phrases for a group of young children.

The game consists of an ever-lengthening set of phrases, each new one adding some new wrinkle. It is not unlike the most difficult tongue twister you can imagine. But worse, players must memorize the nonsense in order to repeat it.

First, select one player to read the phrases and another to go first. The reader reads the first phrase aloud and the other player tries to repeat it. If the repetition is correct, the reader reads the first two phrases aloud and the other player repeats them. Play continues in this manner until the player misses a word or successfully completes the tenth phrase.

Whenever a player misses a word, the next player takes over, and the reader starts all over with the first phrase. I have seen dozens of different sets of phrases for this game, none of which can be identified as the original. The best I've come across is reprinted below:

1. One hen.
2. One hen, two ducks.
3. One hen, two ducks, three squawking geese.
4. One hen, two ducks, three squawking geese, four Limerick oysters.

5. One hen, two ducks, three squawking geese, four Limerick oysters, five corpulent porpoises.

6. One hen, two ducks, three squawking geese, four Limerick oysters, five corpulent porpoises, six pairs of Revlon tweezers.

7. One hen, two ducks, three squawking geese, four Limerick oysters, five corpulent porpoises, six pairs of Revlon tweezers, seven thousand Macedonians in full battle array.

8. One hen, two ducks, three squawking geese, four Limerick oysters, five corpulent porpoises, six pairs of Revlon tweezers, seven thousand Macedonians in full battle array, eight brass monkeys from the ancient sacred crypts of Egypt.

9. One hen, two ducks, three squawking geese, four Limerick oysters, five corpulent porpoises, six pairs of Revlon tweezers, seven thousand Macedonians in full battle array, eight brass monkeys from the ancient sacred crypts of Egypt, nine apathetic sympathetic diabetic old men on roller skates with a marked propensity towards procrastination and sloth.

10. One hen, two ducks, three squawking geese, four Limerick oysters, five corpulent porpoises, six pairs of Revlon Tweezers, seven thousand Macedonians in full battle array, eight brass monkeys from the ancient sacred crypts of Egypt, nine apathetic sympathetic diabetic old men on roller skates with a marked propensity towards procrastination and sloth, ten lyrical spherical diabolical denizens of the deep who stalk about the corners of a cove all at the same time.

Good luck!

LEMONADE

PLAYERS: *six or more*
LOCATION: *outdoors*
EQUIPMENT: *none*
SPECIAL SKILLS: *running, chasing, acting*

LEMONADE is a game I remember playing in kindergarten and first grade. I don't have a clue who invented this acting/guessing game, but it's lots of fun and doesn't require any preparation, equipment, or skill. LEMONADE inspires the sense of fun in every child.

First, divide into two teams. It doesn't matter if a team has one more player than the other. Mark off or determine the boundaries of a rectangular field, enough space for a good game of tag and divide it in half down the middle. At each end of the field is home base for each team.

Choose which team will go first and send both teams to their home bases. The team going first must decide on two things: their trade and where they are from. For example, they could be plumbers from St. Louis, lawyers from Los Angeles, carpenters from New Orleans, or whatever they decide. The trade or profession must be one with which all players on the other team will be familiar.

Then both teams begin walking toward the center line.

The first team shouts, "Here we come!"

The second team shouts, "Where from?"

The first team replies, "New Orleans!" (or wherever).

The second team shouts, "What's your trade?"

The first team replies, "Lemonade!"

The second team challenges, "Show us some, if you're not afraid!"

This back-and-forth shouting should coincide with the walking so that on the last word both teams are facing each other from a distance of several feet on either side of the centerline. Now the members of the first team must act out the secret profession that they have chosen. The second team shouts guesses and the first team responds either with laughter or with horror. They respond with laughter to all *wrong* answers. But they respond with horror when someone from the other team shouts out the correct profession.

At this point, members of the first team break into a panic and try to run back to the safety of their home base while members of the second team try to tag them. Any tagged players join the second team, who then retreat to home base to decide on their profession for the next round.

The game continues in this manner until all players are on the same team.

CHARADES

PLAYERS: *four or more*

LOCATION: *anywhere*

EQUIPMENT: *pencil and paper, watch*

SPECIAL SKILLS: *acting, word building*

Several hundred years ago, CHARADES evolved from an old English game called DUMB CRAMBO (a description of which follows this one) and soared to incredible popularity during the Victorian era. By the late-nineteenth century, CHARADES had become *the* English parlor game; in all likelihood, the game has been played at some time in every English household. Although the game is designed as a difficult guessing game for adults and older children, today's youngsters enjoy CHARADES tremendously through family play.

The English word *charade* is related to the Italian *schiarare,* which means "to make clear or unravel," and this is the object of CHARADES: to figure out a string of words by viewing the silent actions of another player.

CHARADES is a game for two teams who take turns trying to guess the meaning of the charade. Any number can play and there is no equipment necessary. Gather the group in one room and divide into two evenly matched teams. Then select which team will go first and send that team out of the room. Both teams now come up with as many charade titles as there are players on the other team. The titles are written on small slips of folded paper. The charades can be anything the group agrees upon, but are usually limited to the titles of movies, plays, books, or songs.

The teams might decide to use easy charades such as *One Flew over the Cuckoo's Nest,* ones of medium difficulty such as *For Whom the Bell Tolls,* or real stumpers such as *Spartacus.* It doesn't matter what titles they select for the charades, so long as they will give the other team a good challenge. If the charades are too easy or too difficult to guess, no one has any fun.

The teams should now rejoin in the playing room with their slips of paper containing charade titles mixed together in a hat or paper bag. The team going first selects one of its players to act out the first charade. This player takes a slip of paper from the other team, looks at it without showing or hinting about its contents to his team members, then stands to face them. On the word "GO!" the player begins trying to convey the words in the title to his team members *without* speaking, while a member of the other team uses a watch to time him.

Actions and gestures are all the player is allowed to use in conveying the charade to his team. He is not allowed to speak or to use props. The player may try to act out the charade all at once, a word at a time, or syllable by syllable. As he performs his actions, team members shout out responses. The player must do his best to signal which guesses are correct, incorrect, almost correct, and so forth.

When the team finally guesses the complete charade title, the time it took them is recorded on a piece of paper. Then it becomes the other team's turn to guess. Play alternates in this manner until all players on both teams have acted out a charade. Times are added up, and the team taking the least overall time is the winner.

Because CHARADES isn't easy, a set of gesturing clues have grown up around the game and are commonly followed by the acting player. Here are some gestures and signals that should help you convey the words with less frustration and in less time:

Holding up fingers: At the beginning of the game, this signifies the number of words in the title. Follow this with another show of fingers to signify which word you will begin with. Follow this with another show of fingers to signify which syllable you wish to convey.

Clasping arms over chest: This means that you will act out the whole title at once.

Chopping the hand: This means you are going to chop the words into syllables.

Holding up two fingers, then fist: This means that the next two syllables of the word will be acted out together.

Pushing hands away from body: This means that a player's guess is on the wrong track.

Pulling hands toward body: This means that a player's guess is very close and you wish him to continue guessing.

Twisting air with hands: This means that the guess you just heard is another form of the word you are looking for.

Looking over your shoulder: This means you want a player to make his guess into a past tense.

Hand over eyes, looking forward: This means you want a player to make his guess into a future tense.

Thumb and forefinger twisting ear: This means that your word sounds like a player's guess.

Counting with your fingers: This means you want a player to make his guess plural.

Holding up hands, palms out: This means you want the players to stop guessing, because you are going to try another approach or move on to another word.

Touching tip of nose: This means a player's guess is correct.

There are lots of other gestures you can incorporate into your games; the more gestures you and your team understand, the faster you'll solve the charades.

DUMB CRAMBO

PLAYERS: *four or more*
LOCATION: *anywhere*
EQUIPMENT: *none*
SPECIAL SKILLS: *acting, word rhyming*

DUMBO CRAMBO is a very old English parlor favorite, a guessing game in which *no* words are spoken by either of the two teams. In fact, players who speak are put out of the game, a delight to parents from Bangor to Bangkok. The game is actually the forerunner of CHARADES, an easier challenge for a group of young children.

As with CHARADES, divide into two equal teams, then send one team out of the room. This team must agree on a word—any word—as the target for the other team. They must also agree on a clue word that rhymes with the target word. For example, if the team chooses "junk" as the target word, they might select "trunk," "bunk," "clunk," or any other rhyming word as their clue.

Upon returning to the room, the team announces its clue word. This is the last word spoken until the end of the game. Members of the other team now begin guessing at the target word, but not by speaking. Instead, they must act out their guesses. For example, if a player wishes to guess the word "clunk," he must silently pantomime the action of clunking in a manner that some member of the other team will recognize. If the team does not recognize a guess, they should look at the player puzzledly to get him to repeat his guess.

If a player's guess is incorrect, the other team delivers hisses. If correct, they clap. Three incorrect guesses are allowed, but on the fourth incorrect guess the round ends and the other team announces the target word. If the word is guessed before the fourth incorrect guess, the team receives a point. The teams now reverse roles, playing to a predetermined number of rounds or points.

CONVERSATION

PLAYERS: *any number*
LOCATION: *anywhere*
EQUIPMENT: *none*
SPECIAL SKILL: *acting*

This simple game, like CHARADES, requires no props, no special playing area, no preparation, and no skills outside the ability for theatrics. An excellent game for a large family, CONVERSATION will accommodate any number of players.

First, select two players to have the first conversation. These two should leave the room momentarily to decide which famous characters they will play. They should choose a pair of characters with whom everyone else is likely familiar, but the pair need not have actually been associated in real life. For example, you could choose to be Batman and Robin, Henry Ford and Lee Iacocca, Bonnie and Clyde, Babe Ruth and Mickey Mantle, Simon and Garfunkel, and so forth. It is best if you select two characters with *something* in common, otherwise you'll have nothing to talk about.

The two players return to the group and proceed to have a conversation, in character with the famous people they have chosen. If you chose Henry Ford and Lee Iacocca, you should obviously talk about automobiles, trying your best to sound and act like your character would have acted in the same situation.

The other players listen carefully and are not allowed to ask for clues, but must take whatever they get. Once you figure out who the characters are, don't shout the answers. Instead, join the conversation in a manner that lets the two characters know they have been found out. Players are eligible to join the conversation one by one until everyone has guessed correctly or has given up.

There are no winners and losers in this game.

DREIDELS

PLAYERS: *two or more*
LOCATION: *table or hard floor*
EQUIPMENT: *dreidel top*
SPECIAL SKILL: *none*

The game of DREIDELS originated in Germany during the Middle Ages as a gambling pursuit that became part of the Jewish Festival of Lights, the celebration of Hanukkah, and it has been a part of Jewish culture in many lands ever since. The dreidel itself is a spinning top with four sides on which it can land. A single letter is printed on each side, forming an abbreviation for *Nes gadol hayah sham,* which means "A great miracle happened there."

This is in reference to 165 B.C., when the Jews reclaimed the Temple from the Syrians. At the time, their oil lamp had enough oil for a single day, but it kept burning for eight days until fresh supplies arrived and victory was theirs. This miracle gave rise to the eight days of Hanukkah.

There is no skill associated with the game, and there is no betting, in modern times, either. But, if you are Jewish, you might enjoy playing a game with as much heritage as DREIDELS holds. Traditionally, the dreidel was carved from wood or precious metal and engraved with the Hebrew letters for N, G, H, and S.

It is very easy to make your own dreidel. See Diagram 7.1. Just sand down a one-inch cube of wood and drill a hole in the center of one side completely through the other side. Insert and glue a wooden dowel four inches long so that it projects from the other side by half an inch. Use a pencil sharpener or file to make a point on this end. Then paint it and add the letters to the other four sides.

To play the game, each player sits around a table holding an equal pile of counters. These can be beans, chips, pennies, or whatever you have handy. Determine who will go first and the order of play around the table from there.

For the first turn, all players chip in two counters to the kitty in the center of the table. A player spins the dreidel and takes the following action according to which letter the dreidel rests on when it stops spinning. N: no action; the dreidel is passed to the next player. G: the player wins the whole kitty. H: the player wins half the kitty. S: the player must contribute one counter to the kitty. When a player wins half the pot,

Diagram 7.1   DREIDELS

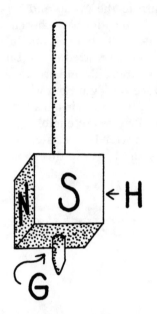

all players must chip in one counter. When a player wins the whole pot, all players must chip in two counters to renew the kitty.

Play continues until one player has won all the counters or until the other players figure they're going to lose eventually and quit early.

MORA

PLAYERS: *two*
LOCATION: *anywhere*
EQUIPMENT: *none*
SPECIAL SKILL: *none*

MORA is a guessing game for two played with the fingers of one hand among a small group. Its origin seems to be Italian. In any case, many Italian-Americans play this fast-paced game of MORA, or FINGERS, as it is sometimes called.

Before the game begins, players should decide how many rounds will be included, or how many rounds a player must win in order to win the game. A player wins a round by correctly predicting the total number of fingers that he and his opponent will throw. Using just the right hand, a player may throw from zero to five fingers (the thumb is a finger in MORA) at his choice.

The two players sit or stand facing each other with right hand raised, clenched in a fist. Simultaneously on a count of three if you wish, the players bring down their fists, call a number between zero and ten, and throw out their fingers. If neither player calls the total number of fingers thrown by the two players, neither wins. But if a player correctly guesses the total thrown, he wins one point.

For example, as their fists are coming down, the first player shouts, "Eight," and the second player shouts, "Four." The first player shows three fingers; the second player shows five fingers. The total number of fingers thrown is eight, so the first player scores one point. If the first player had said "seven," then neither player would score.

THE MATCH GAME

PLAYERS: *two or more*
LOCATION: *table or floor*
EQUIPMENT: *matchsticks or small sticks*
SPECIAL SKILL: *none*

Children love this game as much as adults, and it's simple enough that both can play at their own levels in the same game, with roughly the same chances of success. However, if you're playing with children, you shouldn't play with matches unless you first cut the heads off the matches.

Each player is given three sticks to hold behind his back or in his lap, out of sight of all other players. For each round, players secretly place from zero to three sticks in one fist and hold it over the table. One player is chosen to go first, and he guesses how many total sticks are being held by all the players' fists. Players continue guessing in a clockwise direction until all have predicted the total. Then all players open their hands and the sticks are counted.

There is one restriction on the guessing. You may not guess a number already guessed in this round. The only time a point is scored is by a player predicting the total number of sticks exactly. Near misses don't count. The game continues to a predetermined number of points or rounds. With each new round, play starts with the next player.

CHAPTER EIGHT
Card Games

Next to the bouncing ball, the deck of cards is your best defense against having nothing to do, because there is seemingly no end to the number of games you can play with either piece of equipment. One deck of cards and a few good games can fill an entire rainy Saturday afternoon with pleasant, competitive fun for two players or twelve.

The majority of the thousands of card games in existence were designed for adults, with rules too numerous and too complicated for children to remember. You know the games I'm talking about—Bridge, Whist, and Poker are good examples. However, card games need not be complicated to be enjoyable, by adults or children, and I have collected some of the best of these here in this chapter.

A few of the games, such as OLD MAID and SLAPJACK, are simple enough for five-year-olds to play without adult supervision; many more may be played by groups of children with minimal adult interference. But the majority of these games have been selected because they work very well with players of mixed ages, skills, and interest levels. Family games, in other words.

These are some of the best ways I know to liven those after-dinner doldrums when the excitement of play must be kept down to a dull roar.

OLD MAID

PLAYERS: *two to five*
LOCATION: *table or floor*
EQUIPMENT: *one deck of cards*
SPECIAL SKILL: *card matching*

OLD MAID is a fairly easy game for two to five children, with the simple object of matching pairs of cards. This is a game that children can play by themselves. It requires a standard, fifty-two-card deck *without* one of the queens.

After removing a queen, shuffle the deck thoroughly and deal out all the cards to the players. It does not matter if some players receive one more card than others. The object of OLD MAID is for each player to get rid of all the cards in his hand by matching pairs. Before play starts, each player should arrange his hand in numerical order and place any pairs of cards (a pair of twos, a pair of kings, etc.) faceup in the center of the table. After this, players should mix up the order of their cards.

Beginning with the player to the left of the dealer, each player in turn holds his cards in a fan shape and lets the next player on his left pick one. If the player picks a card that gives him a pair, he places the pair on the table and turns to the player on his left. This player now gets to pick one card, and so on around the table. If a player does not pick a card that gives him a pair, play simply passes to the next player.

The player who gets stuck with the single queen, the old maid, is the loser of the round and gets to deal the next one.

VARIATION:

LE VIEUX GARÇON (THE OLD BOY)

This is a version of the classic card game of OLD MAID as it is played in France. The only real difference between the two games is the one card in the deck that players don't want to end up with. In OLD MAID it is the queen of spades. In this game, it is the jack of spades.

You need at least three players for LE VIEUX GARÇON, and no more than six. Remove all jacks except the jack of spades from a standard, fifty-two-card deck, and shuffle the deck thoroughly. Deal out all the cards to the players, despite the fact that some players may end up with one more card than some other players. This does not matter.

Players now examine and arrange their hands. If a player has a pair of cards (two eights, two kings, etc.), he places them faceup on the table directly in front of him. Once all pairs have been eliminated from all players' hands in this manner, the play begins.

The player to the left of the dealer goes first by turning to the next player and holding up his hand of cards in a fan shape. The other player is allowed to pick one card. If that card brings him a pair, he places them faceup on the table. If not, the card is added to that player's hand, and he now turns to the next player with cards held in a fan shape.

Play continues in this manner until all the cards have been paired onto the table except one: the jack of spades. The winner is the player to get rid of all his cards first, but play continues until all cards but one have been paired. Whoever ends up with the jack of spades in hand is the loser, the old boy, and deals the next hand.

SLAPJACK

PLAYERS: *two to six*
LOCATION: *table or floor*
EQUIPMENT: *one deck of cards*
SPECIAL SKILLS: *card recognition, reaction timing*

SLAPJACK is a very fast-paced children's game, unlike most card games in its use of physical action along with the card play. This, it seems, is what children find so entertaining about the game. It is for two or more players and uses a standard, fifty-two-card deck (shuffle two decks together if you have more than four players).

Shuffle the deck thoroughly and deal out all the cards to the players, who leave them in a face-down pile in front of them. Some players may receive one more card than others, but this doesn't interfere with the game. Each player should arrange his cards in a neat face-down pile.

Starting with the player to the left of the dealer, players in turn lift the top card from their pile and place it faceup in the middle of the table, forming a pile as more cards are added. This action should be done as quickly as possible so that no player, including the one lifting the card, can see its face.

Players should watch the cards carefully as they are added to the pile in the middle. When a jack is placed on this pile, the first player to slap his hand on top of it wins the pile. These cards are then shuffled into the winning player's remaining face-down pile. If a player mistakenly slaps a card other than a jack, he must give his top card to the player who played the card he slapped. When a pile is won, the next player starts a new one in the center of the table.

A player should never give up, even when he has lost all his cards, because he is allowed to remain in the game until the next jack is played. If the player with no cards slaps the jack, he wins the cards and may continue playing. If he misses the first jack to come up, he is out of the game.

The winner of SLAPJACK is the player who ends up with all the cards.

DONKEY

PLAYERS: *three to thirteen*
LOCATION: *anywhere*
EQUIPMENT: *one deck of cards*
SPECIAL SKILL: *card recognition*

DONKEY is a terrific game for players of all ages, particularly enjoyed by the youngest cardplayers. I highly recommend this as a family game. The game may be played with anywhere from three to thirteen players, though the best games are limited to a poker-size group of six to eight. You need a standard, fifty-two-card deck.

First, sort the deck by value: that is, place all the twos together, all the threes together, and so forth, making piles of four cards of equal value. To play DONKEY, you need one pile of four cards for each player in the game. Thus, if you have four players, you need four piles, or a total of sixteen cards.

Shuffle the proper number of piles together and place all other cards aside. (It does not matter which piles you select, so long as there is one pile for each player.) The other cards will not be used during the game. Deal an equal number of cards (four) to each player. Players should pick up their cards and arrange them by number value. The object is to be the first player to get four of a kind.

The game should be played with a lively pace. When everyone is ready, each player selects one card from his own hand that he does not want or need. On the signal "GO!" from the dealer, all players pass their unwanted cards to the players on their left. All players now pick up the new cards and add them to their hands.

Play continues in this manner, with players selecting and passing unwanted cards simultaneously until one player gets four of a kind. This player should not shout in triumph, because only the first part of the game is over—the part that establishes the winner. The second part tests how well the other players are paying attention.

When a player has four cards of a kind, in other words four fours or four fives or four whatever, he should place his cards facedown in a pile in front of him without fanfare, then fold his hands in his lap and wait for the other players to notice. Players should try to "go out" like this without any other players noticing, at least not right away.

As players realize that another has gone out, they place their cards facedown in a pile and fold their hands in their laps. The last player to do this is the donkey, who receives a *d*, the first letter of the word. Keep score on a piece of paper, adding letters on subsequent turns until one player has lost six rounds, gaining all the letters of the word "donkey." This player should be prepared to make braying noises and be laughed at.

SNIP-SNAP-SNOREM

PLAYERS: *three to eight*
LOCATION: *table or floor*
EQUIPMENT: *one deck of cards*
SPECIAL SKILL: *light card strategy*

Also known as The Earl of Coventry, SNIP-SNAP-SNOREM is an easily learned children's game for three to eight players. It uses a standard, fifty-two-card deck.

Shuffle the deck thoroughly and deal out all the cards to the players. It does not matter that some players will get one more card than other players. Now each player should pick up and arrange his cards in numerical order.

The player to the left of the dealer begins the game by placing any card from his hand faceup onto the table. The next player looks to his hand for a card of the same numerical value. If he has one, he plays it on top of the previous card and says, "Snip." If he does not have a card of the same value, he plays nothing and says, "Pass." Play then continues with the next player.

The next player able to play a card of the same value says, "Snap," and the player of the fourth card says, "Snorem." At this point, the four cards are removed from the table, and the player who called, "Snorem," leads any card from his hand as the beginning of the next round.

The winner of each round is the first player able to get rid of all his cards.

Under optional rules, each player also starts the game with ten counters or beads or coins. Every time a player passes, he must contribute a coin to the pot. The winner of each round wins the contents of the pot, at which time everyone must contribute one counter to create another pot to win. In this variation, the winner is the player who ends up with the greatest number of counters.

I DOUBT IT!

PLAYERS: *two to twelve*
LOCATION: *anywhere*
EQUIPMENT: *one or two decks of cards*
SPECIAL SKILL: *lying*

This is an old favorite with our family, as it was always an easy game for children to remember. Not only good for a group of up to twelve children, it's also a game the family will enjoy as a unit. For fewer than six players, you need one standard, fifty-two-card deck. For more than six, use two decks shuffled together.

First, shuffle the cards thoroughly and deal them all out. Don't worry if some players receive one more card than others, because this will not affect the game. Players should pick up their cards and arrange them in numerical order.

The first player, the one to the left of the dealer, takes one to four cards from his hand and places them facedown in the center of the table, announcing that he has played that number of aces. It does not matter whether or not he actually plays aces, so long as everyone else believes him. The object is to get rid of all your cards, so you want to play the right cards when you have them.

The second player must play a number of twos, the third threes, and so on through kings; the next player would continue with aces again. The key to this game is the ability to bluff, because you will not always have one or more of the cards you need when it comes your turn to play. Also, you might want to "pad" your play. Let's say it's your turn and you are supposed to play sevens. You have one seven in your hand, but you also have two eights. You could announce, "Three sevens," but actually play one seven and two eights onto the pile.

If no one challenges a player's turn before the next player plays his cards, nothing happens. You may not go back in time and challenge a previous play. However, at any time, any player may challenge the validity of the current player's cards, at which point they are turned over and examined. If the cards are as they were supposed to be, the challenger must take the entire pile from the center of the table and add it to his hand. However, if the player lied and played wrong cards, he loses the challenge and must take all the cards into *his* hand.

The game continues until there is only one player left. The first player to get rid of all his cards is the winner.

Incidentally, when you use two decks of cards for a larger group of players, you may play from one to eight cards on your turn.

CRAZY EIGHTS

PLAYERS: *three to six*
LOCATION: *table or floor*
EQUIPMENT: *one deck of cards*
SPECIAL SKILL: *card matching*

CRAZY EIGHTS has always been one of my favorite family card games for two reasons: First, it will accommodate from two to eight players; second, there is very little skill and strategy required, so younger players win as often as adults in mixed play. And it's a lot of fun to beat your parents at a game of cards!

Four or five players is ideal for CRAZY EIGHTS. You need a standard, fifty-two-card deck. First, decide on a dealer, who deals out five cards facedown to each player. The dealer then places the next eight cards faceup in two rows of four at the center of the table, as shown in Diagram 8.1.

Diagram 8.1   CRAZY EIGHTS

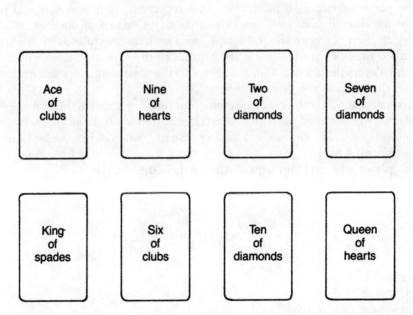

The object of the game is for players to get rid of all their cards by matching them with the top cards in the eight central piles. In turn, beginning at the left of the dealer, players try to play a card. You may place a card on top of a pile with a card of the same numerical value. That is, you could put a queen on a queen, a four on a four, and so forth. If you cannot match one of the eight cards showing, you may play an eight on top of any pile and announce a new number for that pile, whatever you wish it to be. If you do not have an eight, you say, "Pass," and it becomes the next player's turn.

Play continues in this manner until one player has gotten rid of all his cards. Upon shouting, "Crazy eights!" this player becomes the winner, and the game ends. Optionally, points may be scored against players with cards left in their hands:

fifteen points per ace, ten points per face card, and all other cards at their numerical values.

SNAP

PLAYERS: *two*
LOCATION: *table or floor*
EQUIPMENT: *one deck of cards*
SPECIAL SKILL: *card recognition*

SNAP is a game for young children that requires only the ability to read the value of the cards. It is designed for two players at a time, with the object of winning all the cards in the deck. You will need a standard, fifty-two-card deck with its two jokers.

First, shuffle the deck thoroughly, then deal out all the cards facedown into two packs. Each player takes a pack in hand. Then, at the same time, both players turn over the top cards from their packs and place them on the table in separate discard piles. If the cards do not match in numerical value, the game should continue as quickly as possible.

The players continue turning over their top cards simultaneously and placing them on the discard piles until the two cards played match in number. When this happens, the first player to shout, "Snap!" wins both discard piles. The discard piles are shuffled together and placed at the bottom of the winning player's pack.

If the players should call, "Snap!" at exactly the same moment, it is a draw and no one wins the cards in the discard piles.

Players must watch the cards carefully, not only for a match, but for the jokers. The jokers are considered wild cards, which means they may take any numerical value. Thus, players may also win cards by calling, "Snap!" when either one or both of the jokers are turned over.

The player who ends up with all the cards is the winner.

SPIT!

PLAYERS: *two*
LOCATION: *table or floor*
EQUIPMENT: *two decks of cards*
SPECIAL SKILLS: *visual perception and manual dexterity*

SPIT! is a two-player card game of perception and reaction timing, combining elements of SNAP and SLAPJACK into a fast-paced challenge that usually lasts longer than the attention span of either player. You will need two standard, fifty-two-card decks with different patterns or colors so that the decks can be separated easily.

Each player takes one deck of cards and shuffles it thoroughly. Then each player deals the top four cards facedown into a pile, followed by a fifth card faceup on top of the pile. The remainder of the deck is placed next to this pile. Diagram 8.2 shows the setup for the beginning of a game. The object is to get rid of the playing pile—the faceup card and the four cards beneath it—before the opponent.

Diagram 8.2   SPIT!

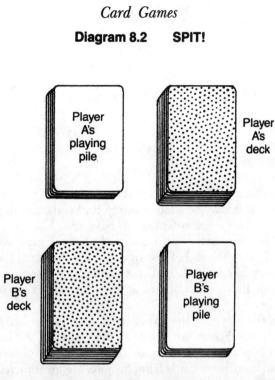

At exactly the same moment, each player takes the top card from the remainder of his deck and places it faceup between the two players while saying, "Spit!" These two cards form the two foundations, and the idea is to move cards from your playing pile onto the foundations. If the top card on your playing pile is either one higher or one lower than a card on the foundation, it may be played there, allowing the player to turn over the next card in his playing pile.

As an example, if one of the foundation cards is a ten, you may play a jack or a nine on top of it. If you play a nine on top of a ten, the next play may reverse the order of the foundation by playing another ten. A foundation may go in both directions. You might start with a four, add a five, then a six, then a five, then a four, then another five.

When there are no more moves available to either player, both take the next card from their remaining decks and turn it faceup on top of the foundation piles already on the table, and play begins again.

When one player has gotten rid of all five cards from his playing pile, the first round ends. Players now sort the cards back into their original two decks, shuffle them thoroughly, then deal out another round. The winner of the first round gets an advantage and a disadvantage: this time he is allowed to deal himself two separate playing piles of five cards each. This means he may play the top card from either playing pile onto either foundation, giving him a greater chance of having the card he needs available. However, he now must get rid of a total of ten cards, whereas his opponent must rid himself of only five.

If a player has more than one playing pile and uses up all the cards in one of them, the top faceup card from a remaining pile may be moved into the empty space, freeing the card beneath it to be turned over and used.

Every time a player wins a round, he deals himself an extra playing pile for the next round. The player who wins ten rounds first is the winner of the game.

BEGGAR MY NEIGHBOR

PLAYERS: *any number*
LOCATION: *anywhere*
EQUIPMENT: *one or two decks of cards*
SPECIAL SKILL: *none*

This is a simple children's game of card recognition that does not require any skill from its players. Still, this may be what children find so fascinating about the game. You don't have to pay too much attention to have fun.

The game will accommodate any number of players, but if you have more than six, use two decks of cards instead of just one. Shuffle the cards thoroughly and deal them all to the players facedown. It makes no difference if some players receive one more card than others. Players do not look at their cards, but keep them facedown in a pile in front of them.

Beginning with the player to the left of the dealer, players take turns placing the top card from their piles faceup into a pile in the center of the table. When an ace, king, queen, or jack is played onto the pile, the next player in turn is penalized and must forfeit a certain number of cards from his pile. He must forfeit four cards for an ace, three for a king, two for a queen, and one for a jack.

Forfeited cards are placed face*down* on top of the pile, and the entire pile becomes the property of the player who played the ace, king, queen, or jack. That player picks up all the cards in the pile, shuffles them, and places them on the bottom of his remaining pile of cards. Then he must start the next round and a new pile by playing the top card from his pile faceup in the center of the table.

The game ends when one player has all the cards. This player is the winner.

CHAPTER NINE
Strategy and Board Games

These are the "brain games," games of mental strategy requiring no physical action or coordination of the players. Many are quick and simple challenges for two players, often improvised with paper and pencil. Others are time- and strategy-consuming, the kinds of nearly silent activity that cause parents to wonder, "What are they up to?"

I have been a strategy- and board-game player for as long as I can remember. I suppose I began with the meaningless TIC-TAC-TOE, but I clearly remember playing FOX AND GEESE, BATTLESHIPS, and JUNGLE CHESS throughout my preteen years. There are many times during a child's life when he wouldn't mind using his mind to think hard if the activity were fun and had nothing to do with schoolwork. This kind of game is the perfect prescription.

So I have collected some of the most stimulating children's strategy games from all over the world within this chapter. A few will be familiar, but the majority will likely be new to you. Don't worry about the exotic-sounding names—I decided not to Americanize them, but leave intact the original names given to the games by various other cultures. All these games are simple, and most can be easily improvised on paper or from wood. But none of them, in my experience, has been easy to master.

Yes, these are all games that children can play. But the strategies they develop and inspire go farther than childhood. In fact, there isn't a game in this chapter that I wouldn't enjoy if you invited me to play.

SPROUTS

PLAYERS: *two*
LOCATION: *anywhere*
EQUIPMENT: *paper and pencil*
SPECIAL SKILL: *strategy*

SPROUTS is a two-player, paper-and-pencil game, of very few and simple rules, that requires surprisingly deep strategy to master. And, in fact, because each game board is drawn differently and at random, no two games ever look alike.

A sheet of paper is prepared with six well-spaced dots, more if a longer game is desired. These six dots may be placed anywhere on the sheet of paper upon agreement of the players. Just make sure you leave enough room between each dot and the edges of the paper to draw several lines. Players decide who will go first and alternate turns until the game is over. In turn, a player must draw a line that either connects two dots or connects a dot to itself in a loop; then he must place a dot in the center of the line he has drawn.

There are only three rules to observe in drawing lines and connecting dots:
1. A line may not cross itself or another line.
2. A line may not be drawn through a dot.
3. A dot may not connect to more than three lines.

See Diagram 9.1 for an example of the board at the end of a game of SPROUTS. If you look carefully, you will notice that every line consists of three dots—one at each end and one in the center. The dots marked X, Y, and Z have only two lines exiting from them, and hence they are still playable. However, there is no way to connect any two of them with a line.

The winner in SPROUTS is the last player who is able to draw a legal line.

Diagram 9.1   SPROUTS

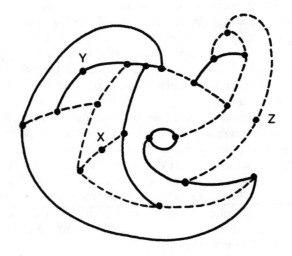

Player 1 __ __ __ __

Player 2 _____

PIPOPIPETTE

PLAYERS: *two*
LOCATION: *anywhere*
EQUIPMENT: *paper and pencils*
SPECIAL SKILL: *strategy*

You probably recognize this traditional French schoolchildren's game as Boxes, the name it is known by in the United States. This two-player game is easily improvised on a sheet of paper.

The board is prepared as a grid of dots—any number the players agree upon will do, and it does not matter whether the grid is square or rectangular so long as it is no other shape. Diagram 9.2 shows a blank 10 × 10 grid, which is the size most players use. You may want to photocopy this grid a number of times before you start playing. Feel free.

Taking turns, players begin connecting any pair of dots with a horizontal or a vertical line. Diagonal lines are not permitted. The object is to "capture" a box by

Diagram 9.2   PIPOPIPETTE

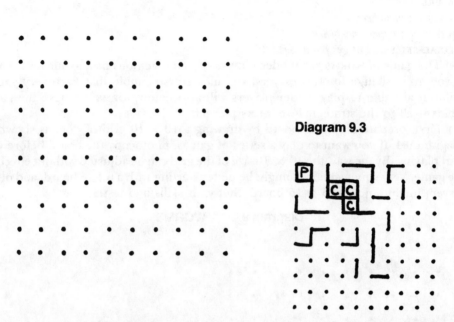

Diagram 9.3

being the player to draw a fourth line that completes that box on the grid. Each player places his initials inside the boxes he completes so that they may be tallied at the end of the game.

Completing a box earns a player the right to take another turn. If the second turn completes another box, the player is given a third, and so on.

Diagram 9.3 shows the beginning of a game between Phil and Chris, in which Phil has completed only one box, but Chris has completed three. Notice that any new lines in the upper left corner will give the other player a chance to make several boxes in a single turn. For this reason, both players will avoid this area for as long as possible.

When the grid had been filled, the boxes are counted, and the winner is the player who captured the greatest number. A very interesting variation—some think, more interesting than the original game—changes just one rule: the winner is the player capturing the *least* number of boxes.

WORMS

PLAYERS: *two*
LOCATION: *anywhere*
EQUIPMENT: *paper and pencil*
SPECIAL SKILLS: *strategy, planning*

The game of WORMS is a modern invention, an ingenious make-your-own-maze-as-you-go challenge for two players. Its rules are so simple that even very young children are able to play. Older players will also enjoy WORMS, because the game molds itself to the strategic level of its players.

First, prepare a playing board by drawing a 10 × 10 grid of dots as shown in Diagram 9.4. If you want to play a series of games, photocopy the board before you start playing. By the way, the 10 × 10 size of the grid can be adjusted without effect on the game. Very young children might be better starting with a 6 × 6 board, and older players might enjoy a 15 × 15 board. Suit your skills and tastes.

Diagram 9.4   WORMS

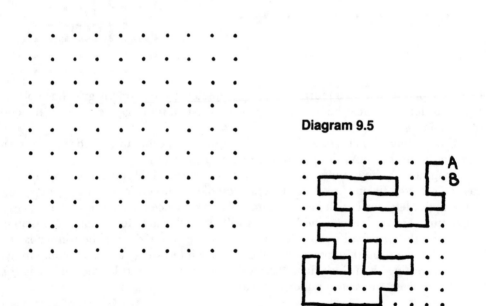

Diagram 9.5

Choose which player will go first. The first player connects any pair of dots on the board with a horizontal or vertical line. (No diagonal connections are allowed.) The second player draws another line that connects one end of the first player's line to another dot. Players alternate turns, adding a segment to either end of the "worm." A worm never has more than two ends.

The big rule of the game is this: no segment of the worm may touch another part of the worm. The object of the game is to force your opponent into a position where he cannot add another segment to the worm without violating this rule. The player who is left without a legal move is the loser.

For example, see Diagram 9.5. There is only one legal move left on the board, from A to B. The player whose turn it is will win the game by connecting those dots.

AGGRESSION

PLAYERS: *two or more*
LOCATION: *table or floor*
EQUIPMENT: *paper and different-colored pencils*
SPECIAL SKILLS: *strategy, diplomacy*

AGGRESSION is a game of territorial capture, and it shares many geometric principles with BOXES and SPROUTS. But this game—most often played in the back of a school notebook—goes a step farther by incorporating arithmetic as well. Thus, AGGRESSION is a bit harder to learn and to master, and older children find it more exciting than the games it builds on.

Although AGGRESSION is usually played by two, it will accommodate more players, who may decide to form teams or alliances. I will describe the two-player version here, but you should feel free to add a third or fourth player, simply taking turns in a clockwise direction.

Part of the fun of AGGRESSION is the pregame phase of constructing the playing map, which is drawn on a large sheet of paper. Players take turns adding a "country" to the map by drawing an enclosed area touching at least one country already drawn. Players are free to draw a country in any size or shape so long as it adds just one new enclosed area to the map. There is *no* strategy to follow in the drawing of the map, because the game has not yet started. No one owns or even intends to own the countries he adds to the map in this preparation phase.

When the map has reached a good size—say, twenty-five countries for two players—each country is labeled with a letter of the alphabet. If you have more than twenty-six countries, start using labels like *AA, BB,* and so on, when you run out of single letters. Again, there is no strategy yet—it doesn't matter which countries get which labels. See Diagram 9.6 for a game board that has been drawn and labeled.

Each player should write down his initials in a corner of the board, and beneath them write "100." This stands for the number of armies each player receives to begin the game. As you use armies, subtract the number from your total in the corner so all other players can see the size of your remaining forces.

Now begins the occupation phase as players seek to capture the largest *number* of countries. For this phase, each player needs a different-colored pen or pencil so that the players can tell which player occupies which countries. In turn, a player chooses an unoccupied country and writes inside its borders the number of armies he is stationing there. If you must use the same-color pen or pencil, at least write your initials inside the countries so you can tell them apart. Once a number has been written on the map, that country is considered occupied and no other player may try to occupy it during this phase. Remember to subtract the number of armies you use from your total of 100. No player's armies on the map may add up to more than 100.

See Diagram 9.7 for an example of the end of the occupation phase of a game. Both players have allocated their total of 100 armies.

Once all players have allocated all their armies or once all countries are occupied by armies, the third phase of the game begins. The player who was chosen to occupy

Diagram 9.6   AGGRESSION

the first country on the map is also the player who makes the first attacking move. This player decides on a country to attack, one that does not belong to him. The country is conquered if the attacking player has armies in adjacent countries that add up to a greater strength than the country under attack.

As an example, see Diagram 9.7. Country A, near the center of the map, is occupied by fifteen armies. If the other player wishes, he may conquer Country A on his turn because his adjacent countries D, E, F, and G have armies totaling more than fifteen. When any country is defeated in this manner, the number of armies within its borders is crossed out. The conquered armies no longer take part in the game.

The game ends when no player can conquer another country. At this time, players total the number of surviving countries. The player with the greatest number of countries unconquered is the winner, even if those countries do not contain as many armies as the remaining countries of another player. It is the number of surviving countries that matters, not the number of their armies.

BATTLESHIPS

PLAYERS: *two*
LOCATION: *anywhere*
EQUIPMENT: *paper and pencils*
SPECIAL SKILLS: *strategy, planning*

The game of BATTLESHIPS is a classic paper-and-pencil challenge for two players. Although war is the subject of the game, players concentrate on strategy, rather than aggression. It offers an equal blend of skill and luck.

First, you need to prepare two identical playing boards—one for each player. I

Diagram 9.7

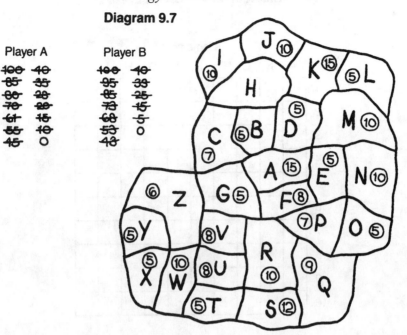

Player A		Player B	
~~100~~	~~40~~	~~100~~	~~40~~
~~85~~	~~35~~	~~95~~	~~30~~
~~80~~	~~28~~	~~85~~	~~25~~
~~70~~	~~20~~	~~73~~	~~15~~
~~61~~	~~15~~	~~68~~	~~5~~
~~55~~	~~10~~	~~53~~	0
45	0	~~48~~	

suggest you draw one blank board and photocopy it before playing. Or just photocopy Diagram 9.8 several times.

Each player now secretly places his fleet of ships wherever he likes within his home-fleet grid. Each player is allowed one battleship, two cruisers, three destroyers, and four submarines. These are noted on the board as B, C, D, and S.

Each battleship takes up four adjacent squares; each cruiser takes up three; a destroyer takes up two; and a submarine takes up one. The squares of any ship must be connected in a horizontal or a vertical line. No diagonals are allowed. Also, ships are not allowed to touch one another, not even at the corners. So you must leave at least one square between all ships. Diagram 9.9 shows one legal setup. Obviously, there are thousands of others.

Once both players have placed their ships, the game begins. Choose a player to go first. From now on, players alternate turns taking shots at the enemy by calling out the names of squares where enemy ships might be located. The enemy responds with "Hit," "Miss," or "Sunk!" A hit means your guess was right on target and your opponent must also tell you what kind of ship you hit; use an *O* to denote this. A miss is self-explanatory. "Sunk" means all sections of the target have been hit; use *X's* to denote these squares.

Players use the empty enemy-fleet grid to record their shots as well as hits, so as not to call out the same square twice. You would record a hit on an enemy's Cruiser by placing a C in the box you called. Once you have located and destroyed an enemy ship, you will know that none of the other enemy ships can be touching those squares, so don't waste your shots on them. Fill them in or X them out.

The first player to sink the entire enemy fleet is the winner.

Diagram 9.8   BATTLESHIPS

Home fleet

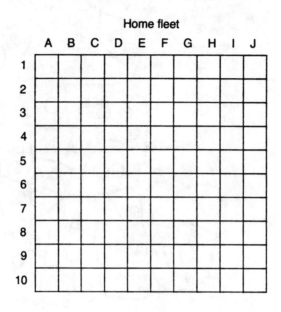

Enemy fleet

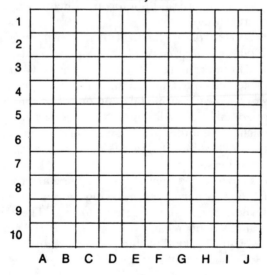

Diagram 9.9   BATTLESHIPS

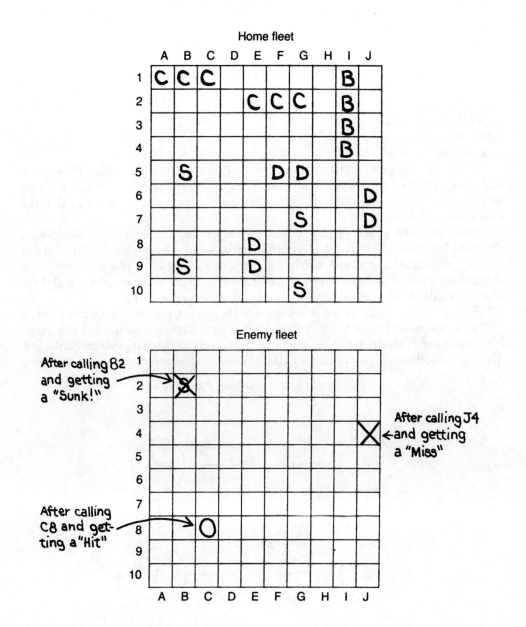

PONG HAU K'I

PLAYERS: *two*
LOCATION: *table or floor*
EQUIPMENT: *playing board and six pieces*
SPECIAL SKILL: *strategy*

    This is a simple two-player game of strategy from China. Actually, the game is played all over the world under many names, including Horseshoe, but the following variation is how Chinese children play. The object is to position pieces so that the opponent cannot move.

    You can make a nice playing board by simply painting or etching the design shown in Diagram 9.10 onto a 4 × 4-inch piece of wood. The circles should be about the size of pennies and connected by the lines as shown. Each player should have three playing pieces that are distinguishable. You could use three red chips and three blue chips, three pennies and three nickels, or whatever you like.

    Set up the pieces as shown in Diagram 9.10, placing pennies on circles marked "P" and nickels on circles marked "N." This is the opening position for the game. Now players alternately slide one of their pieces to the only vacant point on the board. There is no jumping of pieces in this game. If a player cannot move his piece, he loses.

Diagram 9.10   PONG HAU K'I

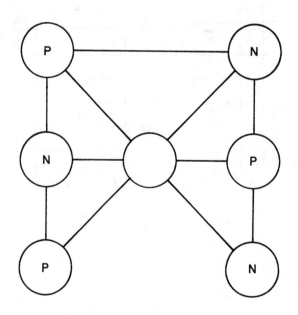

ACHI

PLAYERS: *two*
LOCATION: *table or floor*
EQUIPMENT: *board and four counters per player*
SPECIAL SKILLS: *strategy, planning*

This two-player strategy game, related in certain respects to the Tic-Tac-Toe family, is played actively by children from Ghana. It is played on traditionally carved wooden boards as well as etched in the hard-packed dirt all over the country. This is ACHI's beauty—the game travels well and can be improvised in a moment. Just draw the board in the dirt or on paper as shown in Diagram 9.11 and find small colored pebbles or coins for pieces. Each player needs four distinguishable pieces.

Diagram 9.11   ACHI

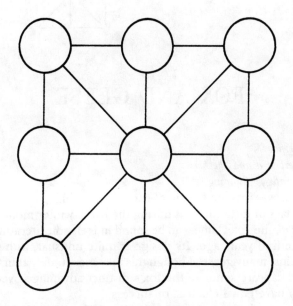

After deciding who will go first, players alternately place one of their pieces on any empty point on the board. There are nine points, in all, on which pieces may be placed. After the players have each placed four pieces on the board, they alternately slide any one of their pieces along a line to an empty point on the board. No jumping of other pieces is allowed.

The first player to get three of his pieces in a row, either vertically, horizontally, or along one of the two diagonals, is the winner.

Diagram 9.12   FOX AND GEESE

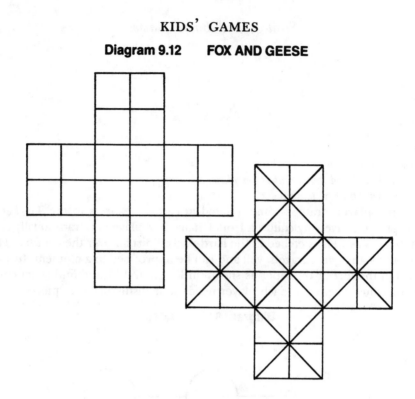

FOX AND GEESE

PLAYERS: *two*

LOCATION: *table or floor*

EQUIPMENT: *checkerboard and checkers*

SPECIAL SKILLS: *strategy, planning*

FOX AND GEESE was invented during Scandinavia's Viking era as a way of passing those long, cold days of little sunlight during the harsh winter months. Its Scandinavian name, *Hala-tafl*, the Fox Game, can be found in Icelandic literature and lore from as long as six hundred years ago. Its design is quite unusual, with two unbalanced sides: one fox against many geese. Though this may seem unfair at first look, the rules of movement and capture simulate the fox's distinct advantage over the geese to a point where both have equal chances of success.

There are dozens of FOX AND GEESE variations, and many variations on the playing board as well. Below, I present the two most common versions of the game. There are two types of playing boards for the first version: with and without diagonals. The board with diagonals makes for a more strategic and challenging game.

The first version uses a special playing board as shown in Diagram 9.12. You may etch this design into a piece of wood or reproduce it on paper or cardboard. Checkers will do nicely for playing pieces. Diagram 9.13 shows the opening position for the game, with thirteen geese against one fox.

The fox is allowed the first move, and it may slide along any line one space in any direction except where blocked by geese or the edges of the board. Geese move under the same rules. Players alternately take turns moving one piece one space in any direction.

Diagram 9.13

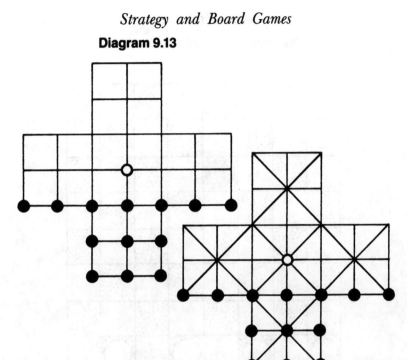

Because there is only one fox against many geese, the fox is allowed to capture opposing pieces by jumping over them in any direction. To be legal, a jump must begin on one side of a goose and end on an empty space directly on the other side. Multiple jumps are allowed. The object for the fox is to capture as many geese as possible.

The geese are not allowed to jump the fox or each other. They may move only one space at a time in any direction. The object for the geese is to crowd the fox into a corner from which he has no move out. The geese win if they are able to trap the fox in this manner. If not, the fox is declared the winner. Players should alternate roles as fox and geese with each new game.

The second version of FOX AND GEESE is played on a regular checkerboard, using only four geese against the single fox. The opening position for this game is shown in Diagram 9.14. Actually, the fox is allowed to choose his own square for the beginning of the game, but it might as well be the one in the diagram.

Again, the fox has the first move. The fox moves like a king in CHECKERS: diagonally one square, either forward or backward. The geese move like normal pieces in CHECKERS: diagonally one square, forward only.

This version of the game uses no jumping and capturing. The object for the fox is to break through the geese and reach the other side of the board. This is how the fox wins. The object for the geese is to block the fox from doing this. This is how the geese win.

Diagram 9.14   FOX AND GEESE

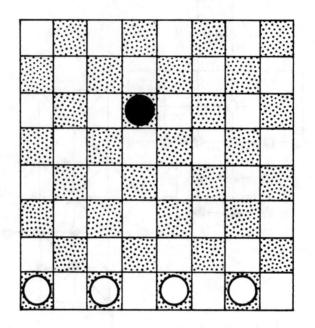

NYOUT

PLAYERS: *two or more*

LOCATION: *table or floor*

EQUIPMENT: *playing board, die, three or four pieces per player*

SPECIAL SKILL: *strategy*

NYOUT is a very popular racing game played all over Korea, where it originated thousands of years ago. It is also played in many other parts of East and Southeast Asia. Although the game is often associated with betting in Korea, it does not require gambling to make it fun to play.

The beauty of this board game is that it is easily improvised and allows for any number of players. Koreans most often play in groups of four, sometimes as two "partners" against the other two. Each player or team must have three or four pieces, known as horses, that are distinguishable from those of the other player or team. Anything will do—coins, buttons, washers—so long as each player has the same number.

The game board is drawn as shown in Diagram 9.15, consisting of a circle connected to the four points of a cross. Using a drill press with two different-size drill bits and a block of wood, you can make a very handsome board. Or simply draw it on cardboard or a large piece of paper. You will also need a single die. (In Korea, flat sticks of wood are used to determine moves instead of the die. The sticks yield only five possibilities, so any roll of six on the die must be rerolled.)

First, throw the die to determine the order of play; the player throwing the highest number goes first in the game. Players should line up their pieces outside the starting circle in the order of play chosen. Players take turns rolling the die and

Diagram 9.15   NYOUT

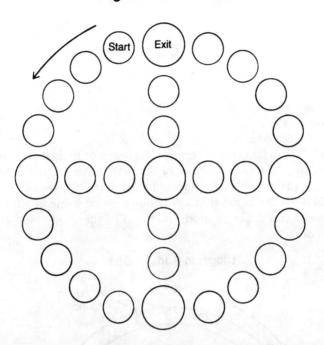

moving their horses the number of spaces indicated on the die in a counterclockwise direction. Remember, a five is the highest roll allowed, so reroll all sixes.

On subsequent turns, a player may enter a new horse into play or move one of his horses already on the board. If you are playing as teams, you have the option of moving your partner's horses as well as your own, and vice versa. Horses go around the circle only once, leaving the board at the Exit. Put these horses aside so not to confuse them with horses that have not yet entered play.

If a roll takes a horse to one of the large circles, the player may take a shortcut on a later turn by moving through the cross. This is an option determined by the player. He may take the route of his choice at any time.

Captures are made when a roll lands a horse on a circle occupied by an opponent's horse. The opponent's horse is *not* removed from play, but is taken back to the starting circle, where it must reenter the board on a later turn. This move allows the capturing player another roll of the die. If you land on a circle occupied by one of your own horses (or one of your partner's horses in a partnership game), the pair may be moved as a single unit on later turns and are immune to capture. In fact, if you land on a circle occupied by a pair of your opponent's horses, *your* horse is returned to the starting gate.

The first player or team to move all its horses around and off the board is declared the winner.

SEY

PLAYERS: *two*
LOCATION: *outdoors*
EQUIPMENT: *none*
SPECIAL SKILL: *manual dexterity*

The game of SEY, a fantastic pastime at the beach or in the backyard for players of all ages, comes from the Dogon tribe, of Mali, West Africa. With almost the entire terrain of the country suitable as a playing board, it is little wonder this type of game was devised there. Many argue that SEY is not a board game at all. I say it is, and a fascinating one. If you'd like to modernize it, I'm sure you could create a playing board from wood.

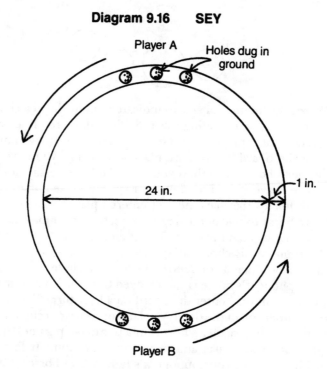

Diagram 9.16   SEY

Diagram 9.16 shows the arrangement of the "board" at the beginning of play. Simply draw two concentric circles in the soil, creating a track several inches wide. Each player sits on one side of the track and digs three small holes within the track, an inch apart and directly opposite those of the opponent. Now you are ready to play.

Decide who will go first. That player is given the *tibi,* a small identifiable stone or pebble, which he hides within a handful of soil. He must now sow part of the handful of soil into each of his three holes, hoping to drop the *tibi* into one of them unseen by the opponent. Try to cup your hand to obscure the action, but you may not conceal it with your other hand.

The opponent now gets one chance to guess which hole contains the *tibi*. If the opponent picks the correct hole, he is given the *tibi* and it is his turn to play. But if the opponent is wrong, the player digs a fourth hole in the sand an inch from the others in a clockwise direction toward his opponent's side and hides the *tibi* again. The only restriction is that he may not hide it in a hole where it was concealed on a previous turn. The player sowing the *tibi* never has a choice of more than three holes.

The game continues in this manner, each player digging a hole closer to the opponent with each successful *tibi* hiding. When one player has used up all the track between his original holes and those of his opponent, the game ends and that player is declared the winner.

YOTE

PLAYERS: *two*
LOCATION: *table or floor*
EQUIPMENT: *playing board, twelve counters per player*
SPECIAL SKILL: *strategy*

It is difficult to know which game influenced which—YOTE or CHECKERS. Both are very old games with similar moving and jumping properties. But while CHECKERS evolved in Europe, YOTE developed in Africa, particularly West African countries such as Senegal, where it is still one of the most popular games. There are hundreds of variations on YOTE; below I present the most common one.

As with many African games, the equipment is easily improvised. Soft ground becomes the playing board; pebbles and sticks become the pieces. Once you know how to play the game of YOTE, it travels wherever you go. Just dig five rows of six holes in the ground, then scavenge for pebbles and sticks.

Of course, it's easy to make the game from wood or simply reproduce Diagram 9.17 on a large piece of cardboard, using different-colored chips for playing pieces. Each player needs twelve pieces.

The game begins with an empty playing board. In turn, players place one of their pieces into any empty space on the board. A player may continue placing new pieces into new empty holes on subsequent turns, or he may begin moving pieces already on the board. A player does *not* have to place all twelve pieces on the board before he begins moving them around.

Only one piece may occupy any hole at any time during the game. A piece may be moved to an adjacent hole either vertically or horizontally. No diagonal moves are allowed in YOTE.

A piece may also jump over an opposing piece to capture it, provided it has a space in which to land directly on the other side. Jumps are made vertically or horizontally, but there is no restriction on which way a piece jumps. It may jump forward, backward, left, or right.

When a player makes a capture by jumping an opponent's piece, he is allowed a bonus capture: he may remove *any* opponent's piece from the board along with the captured piece. The player who succeeds in capturing all his opponent's pieces is the winner.

Diagram 9.17   YOTE

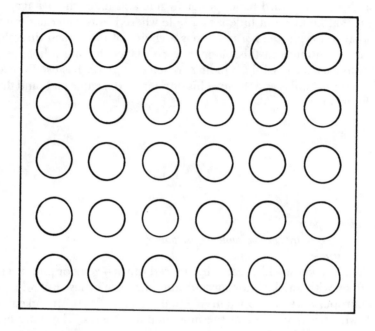

MU-TORERE

PLAYERS: *two*
LOCATION: *table or floor*
EQUIPMENT: *playing board, four pieces per player*
SPECIAL SKILLS: *strategy, planning*

    MU-TORERE belongs to the Maori people of New Zealand, where it has been played on boards of wood and drawn in the earth for centuries. It is an easily learned strategy game for two players, with a most unusual playing board.

    First, draw the design in Diagram 9.18 on a piece of wood, cardboard, or paper. As you can see, there are nine circles on the board: eight small circles around the perimeter called the *kewai* and one large one in the center called the *putahi.* The game begins with each player's four counters on the *kewai* as shown in Diagram 9.18. Only the circle in the center, the *putahi,* is empty.

    Throughout the game, only one piece of any color is allowed to occupy any of the nine circles. Black moves first, and his only choice is to move one of his pieces from the *kewai* into the central circle. He may move a piece from one of the outer circles to the inner circle so long as at least one of its adjacent circles on the *kewai* is occupied by an opponent's piece. Thus, from the opening position, black has just two possible moves: only his pieces adjacent to enemy pieces may be moved into the central circle.

    Players alternate turns, moving a piece of their color. There are only three kinds of moves. The first was described above: moving from an outer circle to the inner circle. The second is just the reverse: any piece may be moved from the inner circle to any empty outer circle. The third is moving from one outer circle to an adjacent empty outer circle.

Diagram 9.18 MU-TORERE: STARTING POSITION

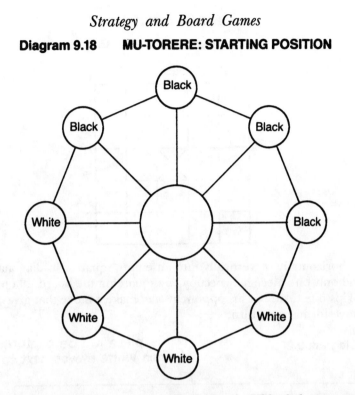

No captures are made in MU-TORERE. The object is to block the opponent, leaving him with no legal move. The first player to do this is declared the winner.

SEEGA

PLAYERS: *two*
LOCATION: *table or floor*
EQUIPMENT: *board and twelve pieces per player*
SPECIAL SKILL: *strategy*

This two-player game of pure strategy was played by ancient Egyptians and is still a very popular game in many parts of northeastern Africa. The size of the playing board and the complexity of the strategy required varies from the 5 × 5 grid described below up to 7 × 7 and 9 × 9 squares. Feel free to experiment with boards of larger size once you learn the game.

First, reproduce the playing board shown in Diagram 9.19, or mark off a 5 × 5 portion of a checker- or chessboard. Each player should have twelve different-colored pieces, for a total of twenty-four pieces (one less than the number of squares on the board). On a 7 × 7 grid, each player needs twenty-four pieces. On the 9 × 9 grid, each player needs forty pieces.

The game is played in two stages. First comes the setup stage, in which players take turns placing two of their pieces at a time onto any empty squares on the board except the one in the center. This central square must remain empty throughout the setup stage.

When all twenty-four pieces are on the board, only the center square is empty. The playing stage of the game begins now. In turn, players move one of their pieces

Diagram 9.19   SEEGA

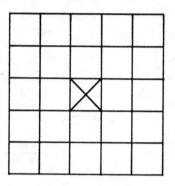

one square horizontally or vertically into an empty square. No diagonal moves are allowed, and only one piece may occupy any square on the board. If a player cannot move, he skips one turn, but his opponent *must* make a move that gives the blocked player a move for his next turn.

Diagram 9.20

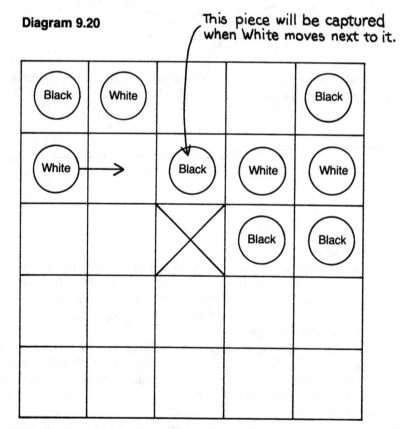

This piece will be captured when White moves next to it.

Single pieces may be captured by "sandwiching" them between two pieces of the opposite color in a horizontal or vertical line. Diagonal lines do not count. For example, in Diagram 9.20, white is about to make a capture. A piece may be moved between two opposing pieces without being captured. And a piece resting on the center square may not be captured. It is possible for a piece to make a move that will result in the capture of two or even three opposing pieces.

Whenever a player makes a capture, he moves the capturing piece one more square in any direction. A piece may continue moving on the same turn so long as it keeps making captures.

The object of the game is to capture more pieces than the opponent does. If a player captures all or all but one of his opponent's pieces, he wins the game. If both players are left with a few pieces but neither can trap the other, the player with the greater number of pieces wins. If both players have the same number, the game is a draw.

SAFRAGAT

PLAYERS: *two*
LOCATION: *table or floor*
EQUIPMENT: *board and four pieces per player*
SPECIAL SKILLS: *strategy, planning*

SAFRAGAT is a variation of SEEGA as it is played by the children of the Sudan. It can be played using the same board and playing pieces, but it is different enough in strategic play to be included here as a separate game.

First, draw a playing board of 5 × 5 squares, or mark off a section of a checker- or chessboard. Each of the two players uses four different-colored pieces, such as chips. As with SEEGA, the game is played with a setup stage during which players alternately place one of their pieces onto any empty square except the one in the center of the board.

When all eight pieces are on the board, players alternately move a piece one square in a horizontal or vertical direction. No diagonal movement is allowed. (Actually, there is a variation in which diagonal movement and captures are allowed. Decide for yourselves.)

The object is to capture opposing pieces by trapping them one at a time between pairs of the opposing color. A piece on the center square may not be captured.

A player wins by capturing all opposing pieces or by blocking the opponents' pieces so that they cannot be moved. If neither player is able to capture the remaining pieces, the player with more pieces is the winner. If the players end up with the same number of pieces, the game is a draw.

NINE MEN'S MORRIS

PLAYERS: *two*
LOCATION: *table or floor*
EQUIPMENT: *playing board, nine counters per player*
SPECIAL SKILLS: *strategy, planning*

This European game, hundreds if not thousands of years old, is still popular all over the world and goes by many names, including Mill, Morelles, and Muhle. It is a purely strategic contest for two players, with no luck involved.

The unusual playing board is traditionally carved into a block of wood, but you can easily improvise the game by reproducing Diagram 9.21 on paper or cardboard.

Diagram 9.21   NINE MEN'S MORRIS

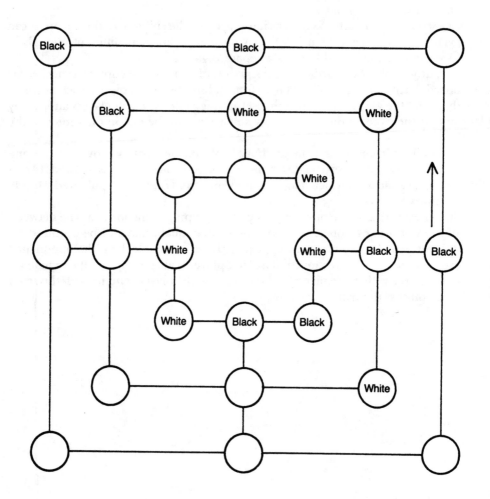

Each player will need nine distinguishable counters, such as colored chips, or pennies and nickels.

The object of the game is to capture the opponent's pieces and reduce his ability to move on the board. To set up the game, players alternately place one of their pieces on any of the board's twenty-four points, indicated in the diagram by circles. When both players have placed all nine of their pieces on the board in this manner, play begins. There are thousands of possible opening setups.

Players alternate turns, each trying to get three of his pieces into a line. A move consists of sliding a piece to an adjacent open point on the board. No jumps are allowed in this game. Three same-colored pieces in a line forms a mill, which entitles the player to remove any single opponent's piece from the board. A piece removed from the board is never reentered. There is one restriction: you may not remove an opponent's piece if it is part of a mill, or three in a row.

If a player forms a mill and removes one of the opponent's pieces, he may move a piece out of the mill on his next turn and back into the mill on the next, thereby forming the same mill a second or a third time. This is legal and entitles the player to remove another of the opponent's pieces from the board.

A player wins by reducing his opponent to two pieces or by maneuvering his opponent into a position with no legal moves left.

DOMINOES

PLAYERS: *two or more*
LOCATION: *table or floor*
EQUIPMENT: *set of dominoes*
SPECIAL SKILLS: *strategy, planning*

The game of DOMINOES is at least as old as the bones of King Tut, who died in 1352 B.C. The young king was placed in his tomb with many familiar objects to guide him on his journey through death. One of these was a set of dominoes, currently on display in the Tutankhamen Museum, in Cairo, Egypt. Still, scholars seem to agree that the game came to Egypt from China. In any case, it was and still is extremely popular in both countries, as well as throughout Europe and South and North America, to which it spread.

The traditional European domino set consists of twenty-eight domino tiles numbered with spots like dice. Each domino has two halves, thus two numbers, ranging from a blank through six. Thus, with each combination from double blank through double six included once, the set numbers twenty-eight pieces, as shown in Diagram 9.22.

There are literally thousands of DOMINOES game variations you can play, and you can find whole books of variations in the library should the following games interest you. I have chosen them for their simplicity as a way of learning DOMINOES play, and for their elegant nature. All can be enjoyed by players of all ages, and I highly recommend these DOMINOES variations for family play.

Diagram 9.22   DOMINOES

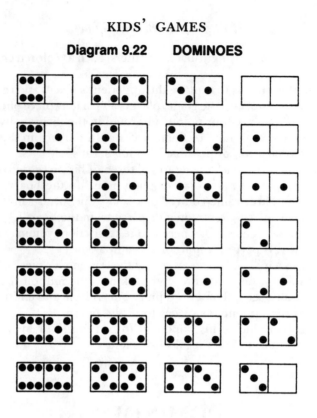

FOURS

FOURS is the easiest DOMINOES game to learn, and the first one I started playing, in my youth. It can be played by three, four, or five players. First, turn all the dominoes facedown and shuffle them around thoroughly. Select a player to go first; then, in turn, all players should draw dominoes from this "boneyard," as it is called.

If there are three players, each draws nine tiles. If there are four players, each draws seven. If there are five players, each draws five tiles, looking at them but not showing them to other players. Any extra dominoes are placed aside, not used during the game.

The object of FOURS is for players to get rid of all the dominoes in their hands by playing them onto the table according to simple rules. The first player takes any domino from his hand and places it faceup in the middle of the table. Then, building on either end of this original domino, the same player continues playing matching dominoes until he cannot make a further play. A match consists of lining up the ends of two dominoes with the same number of spots. Diagram 9.23 shows a partially played game.

Play continues around the table, with each player adding as many matching dominoes as he can to either or both ends of the chain. If a player cannot make a move, he passes his turn. If no player can make a move, players add up the number of spots they are holding on the dominoes in their hands, and the player with the smallest number is the winner.

Otherwise, the first player to play his last domino onto the table is the winner.

Diagram 9.23   DOMINOES: FOURS

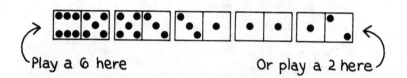

Play a 6 here   Or play a 2 here

BLIND HUGHIE

This is a great DOMINOES variation to play with young children, because it requires no skill. Everything is based on the luck of the draw, so the child is on equal footing with the adult. On each turn, a player will either be able to make a play, or he won't. Children enjoy the suspense, particularly when it's in their favor.

Two to five can play, but the number of tiles drawn by each player varies. For two or three players, each draws seven tiles. With four or five players, each draws five.

Shuffle the face-down dominoes thoroughly; then each player draws the proper number of tiles. No player looks at his tiles, but arranges them in a row in front of him, facedown, without knowing what they are. Choose a player to go first, who picks up his leftmost domino and plays it faceup onto the center of the table. Then, in turn, players turn up their leftmost domino to see if it can be played on either end of the growing chain by matching the ends.

If a player cannot match either end, he places the leftmost domino facedown on the *right* end of his row in front of him. In this way, the next domino becomes available on his next turn.

The first player to get rid of all his dominoes is the winner. If the chain becomes blocked because no player can add to it, the winner is the player holding the smallest number of spots on his remaining dominoes.

THE BLOCK GAME

This popular variation can be played by two, three, or four players. The four-player version is played as a partnership game. First, shuffle the face-down dominoes thoroughly. Each player draws seven tiles into his hand and looks at them. It is asked if any player holds the double-six domino. If yes, that player plays it. If not, it is asked if any player holds the double-five, and so on, until the highest double tile being held is played. If no player holds a double tile, all hands are shuffled and redealt.

The second player selects a domino from his hand with an end that matches the double tile just played and plays it against the side of the starter domino as shown in Diagram 9.24. The next player has the choice of playing a matching domino against

Diagram 9.24   DOMINOES: THE BLOCK GAME

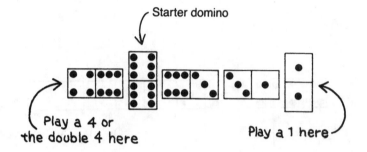

the other side of the starter domino or off the end of the last domino played. Doubles are always played sideways to the chain, as shown in the diagram.

If a player cannot match an end or add a double to the chain, he passes his turn. The object is to play out as many of your dominoes as possible. If a player plays his last domino, he (or he and his partner) scores the number of spots left on the opponent's remaining dominoes. If play becomes blocked, the winner or winning team has the lowest total number of spots remaining and scores the difference between his score and the opponent's.

DRAW DOMINOES

Two, three, or four can play DRAW DOMINOES. First, shuffle the face-down dominoes thoroughly. If two or three are playing, each draws seven tiles. If four are playing, each draws five. The remaining tiles are known as the boneyard, from which players will draw tiles when they become stuck. The object of the game is to get rid of all your tiles.

The game is similar to THE BLOCK GAME in that the highest double held in hand is played first as the starter domino. Then players take turns playing onto the chain, with doubles being played sideways, as in THE BLOCK GAME. All touching dominoes must match, either end-to-end or sideways as doubles.

If a player does not have a domino he can play onto the chain, he must draw tiles from the boneyard until he does. Then he plays this domino. When only two tiles remain in the boneyard, play passes to the next player.

If a player gets rid of all his dominoes, he scores the number of spots left on the opponent's dominoes. If the game becomes blocked, because no player can make a play, the spots remaining are totaled and the player or team with the smallest number wins. The winning team scores the difference between its total and that of the loser.

ENDS

ENDS is a variation for four players. First, shuffle the face-down dominoes thoroughly. Then each player draws seven tiles. The player with the double-six domino is the first player and places it in the middle of the table. The player to his left continues by playing a domino that matches its end.

Play continues in this manner, with each player adding one domino to the chain. If a player does not have a domino that matches an end of the chain, he asks the player to his left for one. This player gives up a playable domino of his choice, if he has one. If not, the next player in line is asked, and so forth until someone volunteers a domino for the original player to place on the chain. Play then continues to the left.

The special rule of ENDS, and the one that children love, is this: if a player asks all other players for a domino to play, but no one has one, the player is allowed to place *any* domino from his hand at one end of the chain, regardless of matching the adjacent one. In this manner, no one gets stuck.

The first player to play all his dominoes is the winner.

JUNGLE CHESS

PLAYERS: *two*
LOCATION: *table or floor*
EQUIPMENT: *playing board and pieces*
SPECIAL SKILLS: *strategy, planning*

Sometimes referred to as The Jungle Game, this strategic two-player challenge is quite possibly older than our Western form of chess. Its exact origins have been lost, but JUNGLE CHESS is definitely an oriental game, possibly a children's variation of Chinese Chess, a game similar in nature to Western chess. In any case, children love this game—not so much for its nicely structured strategy, but because it's fun to imagine the different animals in play. It's also a lot easier than chess.

Ten years ago, I found a commercially boxed set of JUNGLE CHESS in the back of a gift shop in New York's Chinatown area, but I haven't seen one since then. You will likely have to make your own board, but I guarantee it will be worth the trouble.

To make the board, draw sixty-three squares arranged in a 7 × 9 grid as shown in Diagram 9.25. The central square at each end of the board is known as the player's den. Surrounding the den on three sides are traps. Near the center of the board are two six-square sections of water—the rest of the board is land. Color these squares appropriately.

You also need to make pieces. Cut eight small circles from two colors of cardboard. Number them from 1 to 8 and write the name of the animal or draw its picture on each, following Diagram 9.25. The numbers represent the value of the animal in making captures of other animals. Each player should have the following animals: Rat, Cat, Wolf, Dog, Panther, Tiger, Lion, and Elephant, numbered from 1 to 8 in that order.

To begin a game, set up the pieces on the board as shown in the diagram. Select which player will go first, then head into the jungle, where it's not always the strongest who survive, but the smartest.

In turn, each player moves one of his pieces one square horizontally or vertically. No diagonal movement is allowed in the game. A piece may not move onto a square occupied by another piece unless it is making a capture. To make a capture, a player simply moves a piece onto an opposing piece of similar or lesser numeric value. Thus, any animal can capture its mate from the other team or any animal with a value less than its own. Captured pieces are removed from the board permanently.

The object is to be the first player to move any piece into the opponent's den. A

Diagram 9.25   JUNGLE CHESS

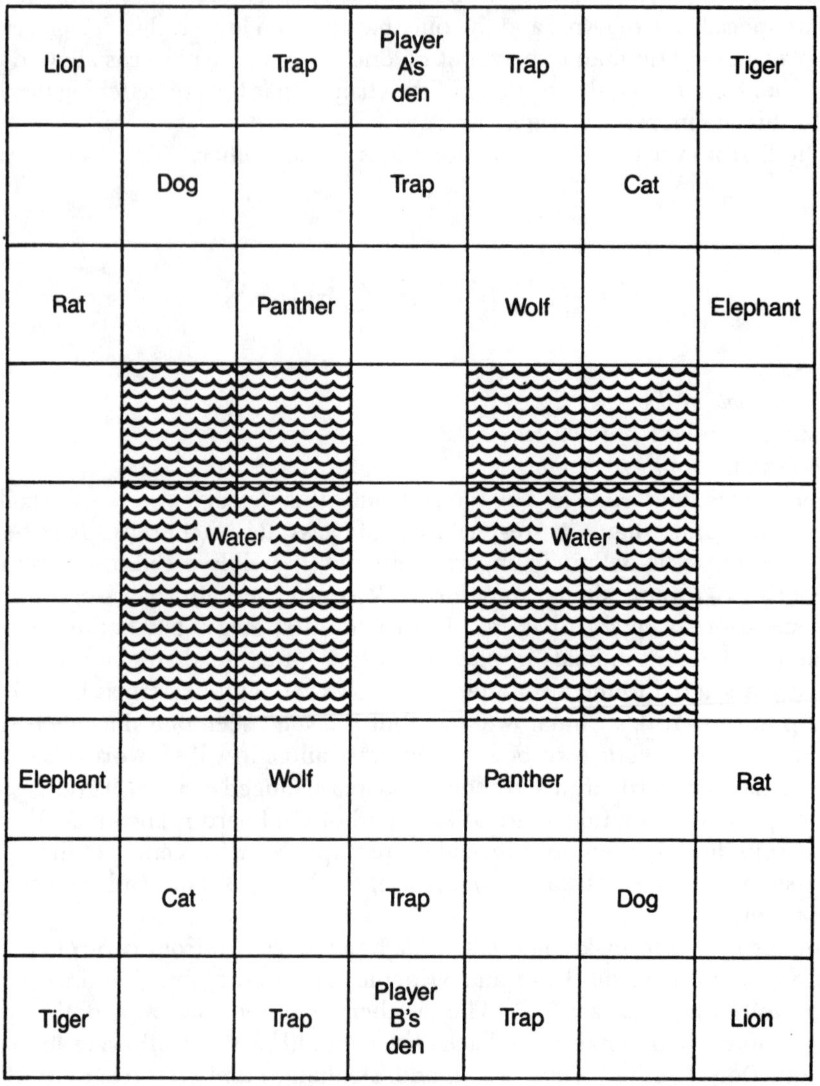

Lion		Trap	Player A's den	Trap		Tiger
	Dog		Trap		Cat	
Rat		Panther		Wolf		Elephant
	~Water~			~Water~		
	~Water~			~Water~		
	~Water~			~Water~		
Elephant		Wolf		Panther		Rat
	Cat		Trap		Dog	
Tiger		Trap	Player B's den	Trap		Lion

piece is forbidden from entering its own den. However, it is wise to position pieces in your three traps. Opposing animals must move through these traps to enter the den. When an animal moves into an opponent's trap, it moves in with its indicated value, making captures according to the rules. But, once in the trap, any animal is immediately reduced to a value of zero, which means that any animal can capture an animal in a trap. Therefore, it is wise to keep animals in the squares *around* the traps.

Only the Rat is allowed to move into and through the water squares. Therefore, the Rat is safe from attack in the water from every animal except the other Rat. Only the Tiger and the Lion are capable of jumping over the water squares, either vertically or horizontally, landing on the first square on the other side. However, neither Tiger nor Lion may jump over a water square that contains a Rat. These big cats may make captures in jumping if unsuspecting animals of lesser value occupy squares by the water on the other side.

One final rule, which no one seems to understand fully: a Rat is capable of capturing an Elephant, but only if it makes the capture from a land square. It may not capture the Elephant by coming out of the water. This strange rule gives the Rat considerable power in blocking the path of one of the most powerful pieces on the board. The Tiger and the Lion are considered as powerful as the Elephant, because they can jump over the water.

REVERSI

PLAYERS: *two*
LOCATION: *table or floor*
EQUIPMENT: *playing board and thirty-two pieces per player*
SPECIAL SKILLS: *strategy, planning*

REVERSI is an old Victorian board game, popular during the same period that parlors were popular. In the 1970s, Gabriel Industries revived interest in the game with their commercially available version called Othello. There are only slight differences between the two games, so if you like one you'll like the other. You may find it easier to buy an Othello set than a REVERSI set, but you can always make your own board.

The board is an 8 × 8 grid, the same as a chess- or checkerboard except it is not patterned with light and dark squares. A REVERSI board has sixty-four squares of solid color. Each player has thirty-two pieces, though not all are used in every game. The pieces are traditionally black on one side and white on the other so that they can be turned over and become part of the opponent's pieces when captured.

The opening position for the game uses just two black and two white playing pieces, positioned on the center four squares. The two white pieces and the two black pieces are diagonally opposite! Black always makes the first move. A move consists of placing one piece of your color on an empty board square so that it "sandwiches" one or more of your opponent's pieces between it and another piece of your color. The sandwiched pieces are considered captured, and all are flipped over to the capturing player's color.

Once a piece is played onto the board, it is never moved to a new location or removed from the board, though it may be flipped back and forth many times. If a player cannot play onto the board a piece that makes a capture, he loses his turn until he can play and capture.

Diagram 9.26 shows white with only one move available and it is black's turn. Black may play on squares marked A through K. Notice that if black plays onto square A, D, or K, he makes captures in more than one direction. Captures may be made vertically, horizontally, or diagonally, and in more than one direction at a time.

The game is over when neither player can make a move or when all sixty-four squares are filled. At this point, players count the pieces remaining of their color. The player with the greatest number of pieces is the winner.

Diagram 9.26   REVERSI

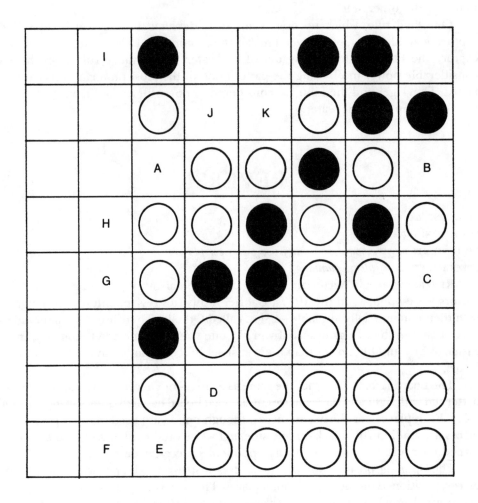

NINUKI-RENJU

PLAYERS: *two*

LOCATION: *table or floor*

EQUIPMENT: *playing board, twenty to thirty pieces for each player*

SPECIAL SKILL: *strategy*

NINUKI-RENJU is a two-player board game with a thousand-year history in Japan, where the game originated. Although the object is simple—getting five of your pieces in a row—the strategy for mastering this game is surprisingly deep. And it is this aspect of "mental gymnastics" that has fascinated the Japanese player for so many centuries.

You'll need some equipment for this game, but it's difficult neither to make nor to improvise. First, you need a playing board, which is simply a grid of intersecting lines.

Diagram 9.27   NINUKI-RENJU

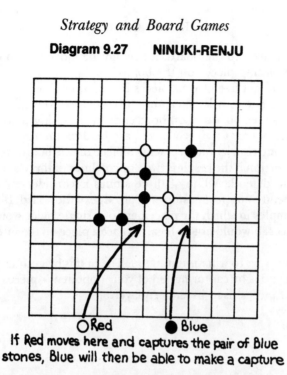

○ Red   ● Blue

If Red moves here and captures the pair of Blue
stones, Blue will then be able to make a capture

Try a 10 × 10 grid to start, and increase the board size as you become more familiar
with the strategy. Either draw the grid on paper or make one from wood or plaster.
You also need playing pieces of different colors, at least twenty pieces per side. Small
colored pebbles are used in Japan, but feel free to use coins, buttons, or any handy
objects.

Initially, the board is empty. On his turn, a player may make just one kind of
move: place one of the pieces from his pile on any unoccupied intersection on the
board. Pieces are placed on the intersections of the lines, not inside the squares. Once

Diagram 9.28

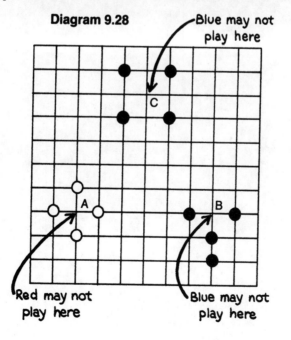

Blue may not
play here

Red may not
play here

Blue may not
play here

a piece has been played to the board, it may not be moved to another intersection. Players alternate placing pieces on the board.

The object is to get five of your pieces in a row, but you may capture opposing pieces during play. The only legal capture in NINUKI-RENJU is illustrated by Diagram 9.27: any pair of pieces bounded on both ends by opposing pieces is captured and removed from the board. Captured pieces are held by the capturing player.

There is just one restriction on placing a piece on the board: you may not place a piece on an intersection if the result is two "open" lines of three stones, against which it is impossible to defend. A line of three stones is considered "open" if it is not blocked at either end by opposing stones or an edge of the board. Diagram 9.28 shows three typical examples in which the placement of a single piece would yield two open rows of three pieces. It would not be legal to place a piece on the intersections marked A, B, and C.

There are two ways to win NINUKI-RENJU. The first is by getting five of your pieces in a row. The second is by capturing ten of your opponent's pieces. There is no limit to the number of pieces used by either player.

CHAPTER TEN
Solitaire Games and Puzzles

Often, just at those times when you are *really* in the mood to play a game, there is no opponent available. Nothing is more frustrating to a game player. When you find yourself in this situation, let Chapter 10 come to the rescue. Here you will find an assortment of games you may play all by yourself.

Most people think of solitaire card games when they think of playing games by themselves, so I've included five very different variations using a standard, fifty-two-card deck. I've also included a couple of strategic one-player board games and several manipulative puzzles.

The following games are dedicated to the lonely game player.

SAM LOYD'S GAME

PLAYER: *one*
LOCATION: *anywhere*
EQUIPMENT: *paper and pencil or playing board, coins*
SPECIAL SKILLS: *strategy, planning*

One of the greatest puzzle inventors of all time was Sam Loyd, a nineteenth-century American. He devised hundreds of puzzles, games, and tricks that have amused us for a century. This one, called SAM LOYD'S GAME, is one of his best strategic challenges.

You may create the playing board from paper, cardboard, or wood by following Diagram 10.1 as an example. It is an odd-shaped playing board, but then, it's an unusual game. Diagram 10.2 shows the starting position for the game. Sam Loyd used pennies and nickels, so we will do the same, indicated in the diagram by P's and N's.

Set up the board with eight pennies and eight nickels as shown in the diagram, leaving the central square on the board empty.

The object of the game is to get the nickels where the pennies are and get the pennies where the nickels are, in forty-six moves or fewer. And you must follow these rules in moving the coins:

1) Pennies may be moved only down or to the right.

2) Nickels may be moved only up or to the left.

3) A coin may be moved one square onto an adjacent empty square, or it may jump an adjacent coin if there is an empty square on the other side. No coin may move diagonally.

If you can complete the puzzle in forty-six moves or fewer, you win.

Diagram 10.1   SAM LOYD'S GAME

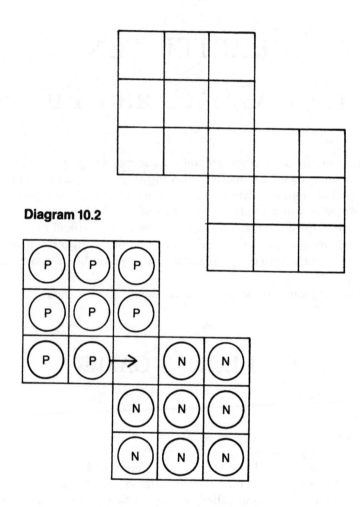

Diagram 10.2

SOLITAIRE: THE BOARD GAME

PLAYER: *one*
LOCATION: *table or floor*
EQUIPMENT: *playing board and marbles, or cardboard and coins*
SPECIAL SKILLS: *strategy, planning*

Who would invent a game called SOLITAIRE that you play by yourself? An eighteenth-century Frenchman who had been given a sentence of solitary confinement in the Bastille prison, that's who. The prisoner had plenty of time to work out the game, and the result is a magnificent pastime that is guaranteed to keep you busy.

The game became popular with French prisoners, their guards, and eventually the rest of the country. Soon it had reached England and was a popular novelty found in nearly every Victorian parlor. The French board is slightly different from the English board, but, either way, the game presents the same exquisite challenge of mental gymnastics.

Diagram 10.3   SOLITAIRE: THE BOARD GAME

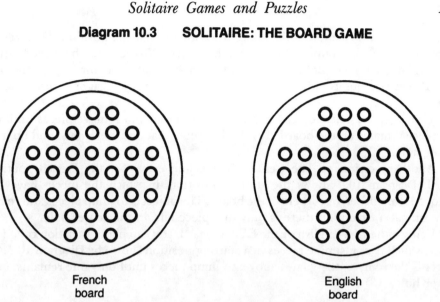

French
board

English
board

You can create a board quite simply by drawing circles on a piece of paper or cardboard and using counters or coins for pieces. Or you can make a nice set from wood with hardly any effort. Using a large, round-pointed drill bit, you can make spherical impressions in a block of wood in one of the patterns shown in Diagram

Diagram 10.4

Eight corners are left empty at start

Diagram 10.5

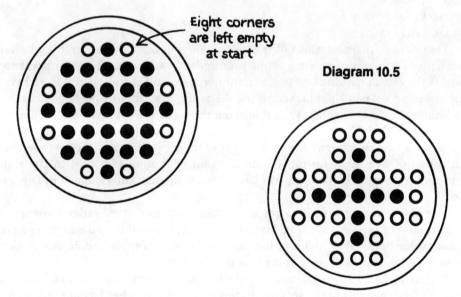

10.3. Then rest marbles in the holes for pieces. Or drill straight quarter-inch holes and use dowel pegs for pieces. With a little sanding and some varnish, this makes quite a handsome game board.

The French board has thirty-seven holes, the English thirty-three. Dozens of variations on play have arisen over the years, based on both boards, but by far the most commonly played one is called The Center-Hole Game.

To set up the starting position for The Center-Hole Game, remove the piece from the hole in the center of the board to create the starting position. Then remove pieces one by one by jumping them with other pieces. No piece may be moved without jumping over an adjacent piece and landing in an empty hole directly on the other side. Pieces may jump either horizontally or vertically. No diagonal moves are allowed.

The object of The Center-Hole Game is to jump and remove pieces until only one piece remains on the board. To win the game, that one piece must end up in the center hole.

Another version of The Center-Hole Game exists for the French SOLITAIRE board. Diagram 10.4 shows the starting position, in which the pieces have been removed from the eight corners of the board. The object is to jump pieces and remove them one at a time until there is only one piece left, in the center hole.

Using either the English or the French board, you can play a variation called The Cross, which uses just nine pieces in a starting position shown by Diagram 10.5. The object is the same as the games above: to jump pieces until only one remains, in the center hole.

SOLITAIRE: THE CARD GAME

PLAYER: *one*
LOCATION: *table or floor*
EQUIPMENT: *one deck of cards*
SPECIAL SKILL: *strategy*

There are so many versions of the card game SOLITAIRE that several books have been written on the subject, each listing hundreds of variations. The game presented below is the one taught me by my grandmother, who said she learned it from hers. I suppose some version of SOLITAIRE is as old as the first deck of playing cards.

Shuffle the deck thoroughly, then deal out the cards as follows. First, deal a row of seven cards, with the first card on the left faceup. Then deal a similar row of six cards on top of the first row, beginning to the right of the face-up card in the first row. Now deal a row of five cards on top of these, again beginning one card to the right. Continue dealing the cards until you have formed the tableau as shown in Diagram 10.6.

The object of SOLITAIRE is to get all the cards into numerical order according to suit by following certain rules. The first and foremost rule is this: you may move a card of lower value onto one of higher value, but not the other way around. In other words, you may place a ten on a jack, but not a jack on a ten.

Begin by making any legal moves on the tableau of cards. You may build on any of the seven face-up cards in the seven columns by moving another face-up card onto it so long as the card being moved is lower in value and of the opposite color. When a card from the tableau is moved onto another, the top card beneath it is turned over for use. See Diagram 10.7 for an example of a partially solved tableau.

When you have moved enough cards on the tableau to create an empty column, only one type of card may be played into that column: a king.

There is a special rule you should know of. See Diagram 10.7. As an example of this rule, the nine of hearts may be moved onto the ten of clubs, bringing with it the

Diagram 10.6   SOLITAIRE: THE CARD GAME

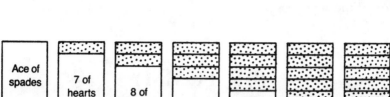

eight, seven, and six. It does not matter if there are cards attached to a card you wish to move. Sequences of cards may be moved as a unit.

Of course, at some point you will become stuck, unable to uncover any more cards from the tableau. At this point, take the remaining pack of cards and begin

Diagram 10.7   SOLITAIRE: THE CARD GAME

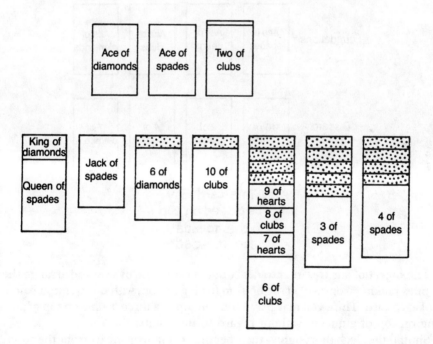

turning them over one at a time, faceup, into a discard pile. Cards may be played from the discard pile to the tableau at any time, but only the top card may be used.

When you uncover the aces, they should be moved into a row all by themselves above the tableau. It is on these aces that you hope to build all the other cards in order and by suit. Cards may be played onto the aces in ascending order only, and, of course, must now agree in suit.

You may go through the pack of cards only once. When you have no further legal moves, the game ends. The only way to win is by ending up with all the cards sorted by suit on top of the aces.

SIR TOMMY

PLAYER: *one*
LOCATION: *table or floor*
EQUIPMENT: *one deck of cards*
SPECIAL SKILL: *strategy*

Card games that you play alone belong to the family called solitaire in the United States and patience in England and Europe. SIR TOMMY is an English game, quite possibly the first one-player card game, and the ancestor of all the others. It requires a standard, fifty-two card deck.

Diagram 10.8   SIR TOMMY

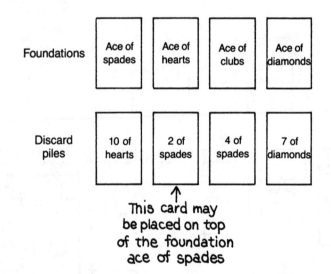

The object of SIR TOMMY is to deal out the cards one by one and arrange them in four piles ranking from ace on the bottom to king on top, with no attention paid to the suit of each card. Thus, you may play a four on top of a three, a nine on top of an eight, a king on top of a queen, without regard to their suits.

Shuffle the deck thoroughly, then begin turning over cards from the top of the deck (known as the stock) one at a time. When you turn up an ace, place it faceup on the table to form one foundation. Eventually, you will have four foundations, one for each ace. When you turn up a card other than an ace, you may place it faceup in a waste pile. You may create as many as four waste piles, and you may place an unusable card on the waste pile of your choice.

The top card from any waste pile may be moved to any foundation when it is needed. Thus, the game becomes a matter of juggling cards on the waste piles so as not to bury the low-value cards early in the game. Diagram 10.8 shows a game in which the four aces have been uncovered.

The game is won if you succeed in forming the four foundations all the way from ace through king. You may go through the deck (stock) only once.

PUSS IN THE CORNER

PLAYER: *one*
LOCATION: *table or floor*
EQUIPMENT: *one deck of cards*
SPECIAL SKILL: *strategy*

This variation of SIR TOMMY uses most of the same rules but is more difficult to win. It also uses a standard, fifty-two card deck.

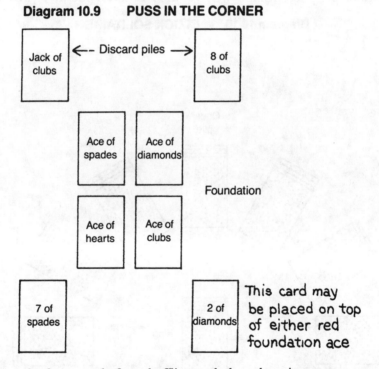

Diagram 10.9   PUSS IN THE CORNER

Remove the four aces before shuffling and place them in a square arrangement. This forms the foundation. Shuffle the deck thoroughly, then begin turning over cards from the top of the deck one at a time. Your task is to build the foundations from ace through king using cards of the same color. That is, a two of diamonds could be played on the ace of diamonds or the ace of hearts.

Any card that is not immediately playable onto the foundation is placed faceup on one of four discard piles arranged at the corners of the foundation as shown in Diagram 10.9. When a card on top of a discard pile becomes playable onto the foundation, it may be moved there.

To win the game, you must end up with four foundation piles complete from aces through kings. Each pile must contain only cards of the same color.

CLOCK SOLITAIRE

PLAYER: *one*
LOCATION: *table or floor*
EQUIPMENT: *one deck of cards*
SPECIAL SKILL: *strategy*

CLOCK SOLITAIRE, also known as Four of a Kind and Hidden Cards, is an easy solitaire version to learn, because there is no skill involved in the game. Success is all a matter of luck, which makes the game enjoyable by young children, especially those who have just learned their numbers. You need a standard, fifty-two-card deck.

Shuffle the deck thoroughly and deal out all the cards facedown into thirteen piles, four cards per pile. Arrange twelve of the face-down piles in a circle imitating

Diagram 10.10   CLOCK SOLITAIRE

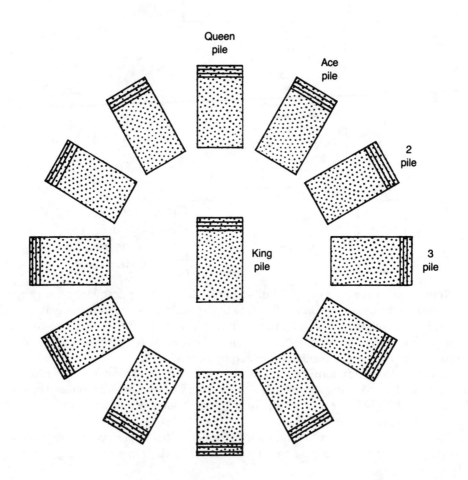

the hours on a clock, and place the last pile in the center of the circle, as shown in Diagram 10.10. This last pile is known as the king pile. The other piles are identified as the 1 pile, the 2 pile, and so forth as if going around the face of a clock. Thus, the jack pile is at the 11 o'clock position and the Queen pile at 12 o'clock.

To begin the game, turn over the top card in the king pile in the center of the circle and place it faceup beneath the pile where it belongs. For example, if you turn up a 7, place it beneath the pile at the 7 o'clock position. Then turn over the top card of *that* pile, in this case the 7 pile. Again, place the card faceup beneath the pile where it belongs. Let's say you turn over a queen from the top of the 7 pile. Place the queen faceup beneath the queen pile, at the 12 o'clock position.

Continue turning over cards and moving them to the bottoms of the piles where they belong until either you have turned up all four kings, which ends the game, or you succeed in turning over all the cards in the piles from ace through queen, which wins the game.

ELEVENS

PLAYER: *one*
LOCATION: *table or floor*
EQUIPMENT: *one deck of cards*
SPECIAL SKILLS: *strategy, addition*

This one-player card game is much more strategic than most other SOLITAIRE games, requiring some planning and the arithmetic ability to add values of cards together. You need a standard, fifty-two-card deck.

Shuffle the deck thoroughly, then deal the cards into four columns and three rows as shown in Diagram 10.11. Each pile should contain three cards face down and the top or fourth card face up. You will be left with four extra cards. Place these extras to the side, facedown.

The object of the game is to remove all cards from the tableau by forming pairs of cards that total eleven. An ace and a 10 make a pair, so do 9 and 2, 8 and 3, 7 and 4, and 6 and 5. You may remove any of these pairs of cards at any time. Place them in a discard pile above the tableau. Kings, queens, and jacks are not used in the play of the game, so remove any face cards you see to the discard pile and turn over the top cards beneath them.

When you have removed all four cards from a pile and created an empty space on the tableau, it may be filled with the top card from your extra pile of four cards, faceup. If you have already exhausted the extra pile, you must leave the empty spaces empty. You may not move cards from the tableau into the empty spaces.

If you succeed in removing all cards from the tableau into the discard pile, you win.

Diagram 10.11   ELEVENS

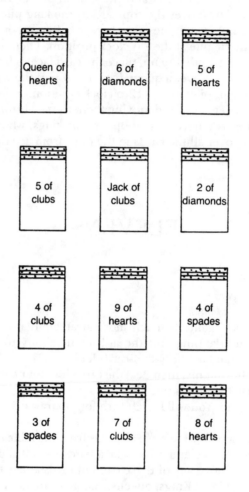

BEAT THE CLOCK

PLAYERS: *one or more*
LOCATION: *table or floor*
EQUIPMENT: *two dice*
SPECIAL SKILL: *none*

The object of this simple yet amusing pastime is to roll the numbers one through twelve consecutively using just twelve throws of the dice. I know this sounds improbable, but the fact that you use two dice makes it possible. Obviously, it is named for the twelve numbers on the face of a clock.

To begin, simply start rolling the dice. When you roll a one, the game begins and you try to roll a two on your next turn. On each roll of the dice, you may select the number on either die or you may add them together and use the total as your number. Thus, on a roll of two and three, you may use the number two, three, or five.

Each time you fail to roll the needed number, you must start again trying to roll a one. See how long it takes you to roll all twelve numbers consecutively and beat the clock.

TANGRAMS

PLAYER: *one*
LOCATION: *table or floor*
EQUIPMENT: *tangram set or cardboard and scissors*
SPECIAL SKILL: *creativity*

Tangrams is a puzzle/game that originated in China almost two thousand years ago, though the history is quite fuzzy. One account of its invention has it that a man named Tan was making a beautiful ceramic tile when he dropped it on the floor, shattering the tile into seven pieces. At first, he was heartbroken. But after fiddling with the pieces in an attempt to repair the tile, he found he could imitate all sorts of shapes: houses, boats, trees, animals—and on it went.

Although the above explanation is unlikely the true story, it is fanciful enough for me to believe until a better one comes along.

As it turns out, there are no fewer than sixteen hundred designs that can be created with a single tangram set, of seven pieces. The object of the game is to use your imagination to create silhouettes of recognizable objects using *all* seven pieces. This is the one and only strict rule of tangram play: each figure you design must use no more and no less than the full set of seven pieces.

If you can't find a set of TANGRAMS in the stores, the pieces are not difficult to

Diagram 10.12   TANGRAMS

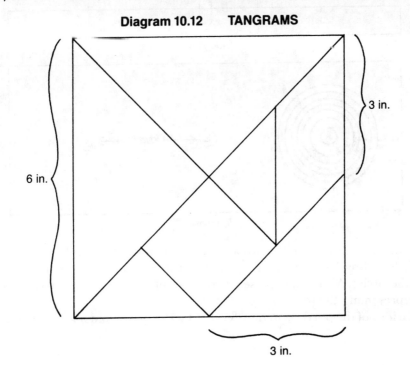

3 in.

6 in.

3 in.

create from wood or stiff cardboard. Diagram 10.12 is a full-size representation that you may trace, copy, and cut out. Try to measure and cut the pieces as exactly as possible for the best fit.

THE DEVIL'S TOWER

PLAYER: *one*
LOCATION: *anywhere*
EQUIPMENT: *playing board or cardboard, and pencil*
SPECIAL SKILLS: *strategy, planning*

Also known as The Tower of Hanoi, The Devil's Puzzle, and several other names, THE DEVIL'S TOWER is a very old puzzle that can occupy your mind for hours with its treachery. You will need to make the puzzle for yourself, but this is easily done.

If you have access to a woodshop, you can make the puzzle by cutting seven disks, each slightly smaller than the last. Drill a hole through the centers of the disks and drill three holes into a block of wood. Place three-inch dowels into the holes and place the stack of disks, largest disk first, onto one of the dowels so that you have a puzzle resembling that in Diagram 10.13.

Diagram 10.13   THE DEVIL'S TOWER

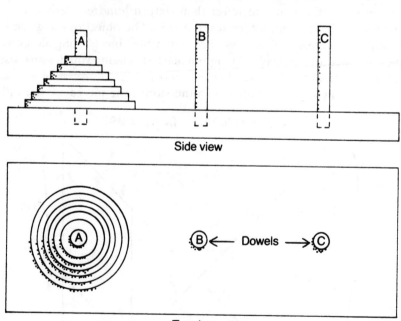

Side view

Top view

If you can't make it out of wood, cut the circles out of cardboard. Instead of dowels, draw three large circles on a piece of cardboard and place the stack of disks on one of the circles. Also, you may use seven consecutively numbered playing cards in a stack representing the tower.

The idea of the puzzle is to transfer the stack of disks from one dowel or circle to another, usually from one end to the other, using the central dowel or circle only as a temporary holding place for the disks.

The disks must be moved according to this one simple rule: no disk may ever be placed on top of a smaller disk. You may transfer the disks from one stack to the next at will, moving them back and forth. And you may place the smallest disk directly on top of the largest one if you like. But never the other way around: you may not place a disk on top of a smaller disk.

You may move only one disk at a time. How many moves will it take to transfer the disks from Stack A to Stack C?

MAGIC SQUARES

PLAYERS: *one or two*
LOCATION: *anywhere*
EQUIPMENT: *playing board, or paper and pencil*
SPECIAL SKILLS: *arithmetic, strategy, planning*

The pastime of MAGIC SQUARES has intrigued mathematicians, scientists, teachers, and other people of knowledge since ancient Egyptian and Greek civilizations. The origins of MAGIC SQUARES lie shrouded in astrological, supernatural, and religious ceremonies, because the ancients believed that the unusual arrangements of numbers of a MAGIC SQUARE could be tapped for its magical powers.

My interest in MAGIC SQUARES is hardly supernatural. The child taps his own

Diagram 10.14   MAGIC SQUARES

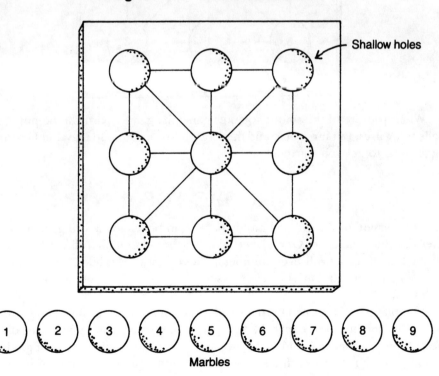

powers when playing with this game, powers much deeper than the ability to add numbers.

It's very easy to make your own playing board from paper, and cut out playing pieces and mark them with a pencil. It's also very easy to make a handsome game board from wood. Use a piece of wood four inches by four inches. Drill nine shallow impressions in the wood as illustrated by Diagram 10.14. You don't need to drill holes *through* the wood; just drill deep enough so that the impressions you create will keep marbles from rolling off the board. Paint lines connecting the squares as shown.

Now paint the numbers 1 through 9 on nine small marbles and you're ready to play. The object is to arrange the marbles on the board so that all rows, columns, and both diagonal lines add up to fifteen. One solution is shown in Diagram 10.15. In fact, this is the only solution except for six mirror images and rotations of itself. Even once you've looked at the solution, it's not a simple matter to reconstruct it on the board.

Diagram 10.15

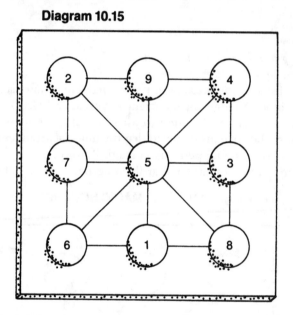

When you tire of the MAGIC SQUARES game, its game board can be put to other challenging uses. I'm sure you could think of your own games to play, but here are two suggestions to get you started.

TIC-TAC-TOE

This version of the old and moldy paper-and-pencil game brings new life to an otherwise dull challenge. One player takes all the odd-numbered marbles, and the other takes all those with even numbers. The one with the odd marbles goes first, because he has an extra marble. He plays any of his marbles onto any open space on the board.

The players take turns alternately placing a marble from their hands onto the board, with the object of being the first player to create a row, column, or diagonal line of three marbles that add up to fifteen. Players should alternate using odd- and even-numbered marbles each game so that the same player doesn't always go first.

NINE HOLES

The playing board for NINE HOLES consists of a grid of 3 × 3 points connected by lines. There are no diagonal lines in the game, so you'll have to imagine the board looks like Diagram 10.16. This game is for two players, each of whom has three marbles distinguishable by color.

Diagram 10.16   NINE HOLES

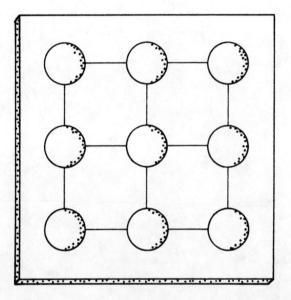

The game begins with an empty board. In turn, players place one of their marbles on any open point. When all six marbles are on the board, players take turns moving their marbles to adjacent points. The winner is the player who maneuvers his three marbles into a vertical or a horizontal line.

INDEX
Numbers of Players

ONE-PLAYER GAMES

TWO-PLAYER GAMES

THREE-PLAYER GAMES

FOUR-PLAYER GAMES

FIVE-PLAYER GAMES

SIX-PLAYER GAMES

EIGHT-PLAYER GAMES

TEN-PLAYER GAMES

About the Author

PHIL WISWELL has been an eclectic game player all his life, which drew him to *Games* magazine in 1977. There he spent four years as the Game & Book Review Editor. Duties included editing/writing game and book reviews, editing logic puzzles, conceiving feature stories, and translating all types of traditional games and their rules into magazine format. That experience is invaluable to this project.

For four years, Wiswell has been a free-lance writer, specializing in games, computers, and technology. He lives on a dirt road in Cross River, New York, with his wife and three children (the playtesters).

INDEX